Horizons

Penmanship

2

Teacher's Guide

Author:

Mary Ellen Quint, Ph.D.

Editor:

Alan Christopherson, M.S.

Alpha Omega Publications, Inc. • Rock Rapids, IA

Copyright © MM

Alpha Omega Publications, Inc.
804 N. 2nd Ave. E.
Rock Rapids, IA 51246-1759
All rights reserved.

Scripture taken from the HOLY BIBLE, NEW INTERNATIONAL VERSION, Copyright 1973, 1978, 1984 by International Bible Society. Used by permission of Zondervan Publishing House

Printed in the United States of America

ISBN 978-0-7403-0210-7

Table of Contents

iv

Introduction

General Introduction

"Whatever you do, work at it with all your heart, as working for the Lord, not for men." (Colossians 3:23).

By the second grade, children have learned a sense of the importance of writing legibly. They know enough words to write notes to those who are close to them. They have experienced the joy of being able to share a story, a poem, or the Word of God with others through writing.

Stress the importance of continued practice to learn to write well. Remind them that the message they have for others will not get through if the person cannot read that message because of illegible handwriting. Tell the children that this year, the quotes they will write and the words they will use demand good concentration and their best writing skills. Explain that about half way through the year, the class will begin to learn cursive writing, another skill that is only acquired through careful practice.

Handwriting time should be a relaxed time, not a stressful time. Always give adequate "warm-up" time before writing, especially in the beginning when children are learning the formation of new letters. Have them form letters in the air, on their desks, etc. as an introductory activity each day until they are sure of the letter formations and the correct starting and ending points. After doing some initial warm up exercises, try adding some soft, light classical music in the background while the children practice.

The total time for handwriting class should not be more than 10–15 minutes at one sitting. Children will tire and they will not be able to do their best. Teach the children simple hand exercises to use (shaking of hands, moving them around) if they get tired.

Cursive readiness should be a part of the curriculum from the beginning of the year.

Suggestions for cursive preparation:

1. Begin the visual preparation for cursive writing immediately by displaying a chart of the cursive alphabet alongside the manuscript chart.
2. After six weeks of school, make a chart of names. Write each child's name in both manuscript and cursive on the chart and display. Have the children find their names and discuss which letters are the same and which are different.
3. Have individual letter cards representing both the manuscript and the cursive letters available for the children to use during free time. They can play matching games with them and begin to visualize words written in cursive.
4. After ten weeks, begin labeling furniture and other items in the room with cards that include the name of the item in both manuscript and cursive.
5. After twelve weeks of school begin writing the weekly quote or verse out in cursive as well as manuscript. Have the children read and compare the two.

6. In week fifteen, copy the cursive alphabet guide for each child and, if possible, laminate it. Place it in the child's writing folder to be used as a reference.

7. In the sixteenth week, cursive writing is introduced. By this time, it is hoped that the children will have gained visual recognition of the letters and the transition to writing cursive with understanding will be easier.

8. Have individual name cards and alphabet reference guides for the children at their desks when you begin to introduce cursive.

"Exploring" Great Handwriting

God tells us to do everything we do in the name of Jesus. That means we do our best at each task he gives us at home or in school. It includes learning how to print and write well.

Our friends, Julie and Josh, are here to help you learn why handwriting is important and how you can do your best.

Do you like to send special messages to your friends and your family? Do you like to surprise people with stories or poems? If you know how to write well, you can do all of these and make people very happy.

Divers Julie and Josh are ready to help you explore ways to good handwriting this year. You'll travel with them through the alphabet. You'll learn to write words praising God in His Creation and special poems that you can share with those you love, with friends, or even with strangers who need some love and encouragement in their lives.

On the first few pages, you will find some tips for good handwriting: how to sit, how to place your paper on your desk or table, how to hold your pencil, and how to form each letter of the alphabet correctly. These tips are the first stages of your trip to good handwriting. Come back to these pages often until you are sure you know exactly what to do.

This year, you will review your "manuscript" print and then venture into "cursive" writing. Learning cursive is very important for all of your life. Watch how many times people you know use cursive to sign forms or write letters. See if you can find other ways people use cursive.

Each day you will have a handwriting lesson. For three days each week, you will practice forming letters and words. On the fourth day, you will practice a poem or a Bible verse. On the fifth day, you will use your best penmanship to copy the poem or verse onto a specially-designed page. You can use these special pages to decorate your room, to give as a gift to someone you love, or to send to someone. You will think of many ways to use these special pages.

Each day of the week, you will be giving God your best efforts in all you do. So get yourself ready to explore the different depths to great handwriting.

Correct Right-Handed Position

Paper is placed on an angle to the left. Left hand steadies the paper and moves it up as you near the bottom of the page. Right hand is free to write.

Correct Left-Handed Position

Paper is placed on an angle to the right. Right hand steadies the paper and moves it up as you near the bottom of the page. Left hand is free to write. Watch hand positions carefully as shown in the picture.

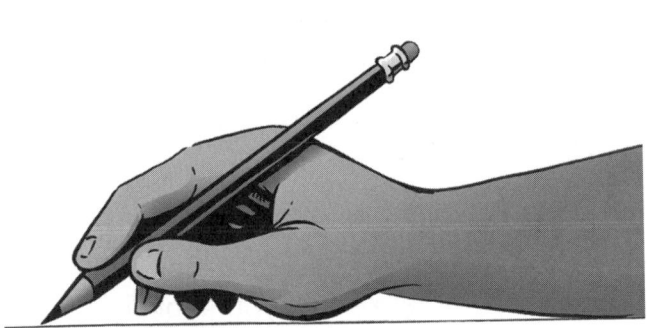

Correct Hand and Pencil Position

Hold the pencil loosely about 1/2" to 1" above the sharpened point. Hold it between your thumb and index (pointer) finger. Let it rest on your middle finger. Do not grip the pencil tightly or your hand will become very tired. Do not let your hand slip down to the sharp point or you will have difficulty writing properly.

Correct Posture

Sit up tall, leaning slightly forward but not bending over your desk. Have your feet flat on the floor. Both arms will rest on the desk. Hold the paper with your free hand.

$\mathscr{A}a$ $\mathscr{B}b$ $\mathscr{C}c$ $\mathscr{D}d$

Correct Spacing

When practicing your letters separately and, later, when writing your words, use your index (pointer) finger as a guide. Continue to do this until you can easily see the space you need between words without using your finger.

Guide Lines

The blue top and bottom lines and the dotted red centerline will be your guides for letter formations. Some letters are one space tall, others are two spaces tall. Some letters like a **p** are two spaces tall but begin in bottom space and drop down one space below the bottom guideline. A few letters are three spaces tall. They use both spaces between the guidelines and drop one space below the line.

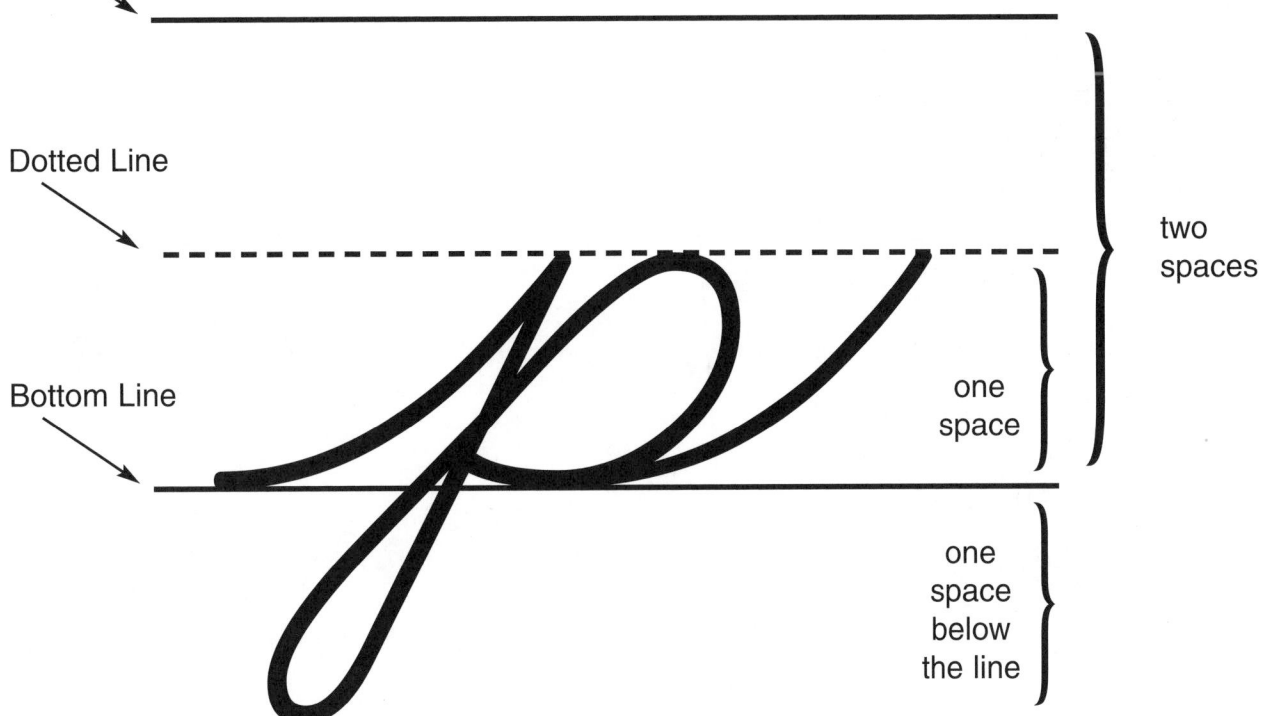

Top Line

Dotted Line

Bottom Line

two spaces

one space

one space below the line

Poem and Bible Verse Pages

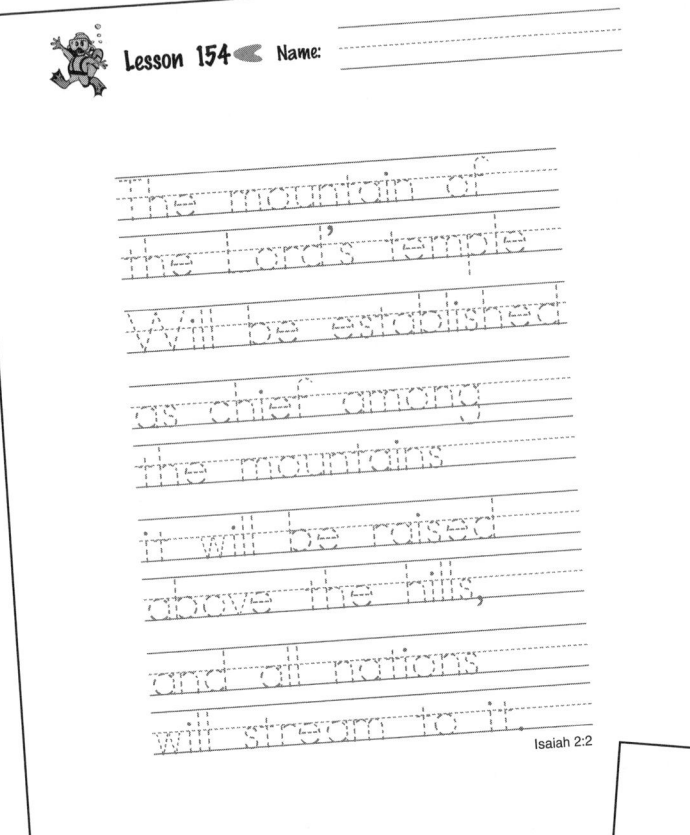

One very special thing you can do once you have learned to write is to share God's Word with others.

Through out the book you will have your own special poem or Bible verse for each week. After practicing the letters and words needed for three days, you will be able to practice your poem or verse on the fourth day.

You will also have a special page on the fifth day of the week where you will copy the poem or verse, decorate it and decide how you will share it with someone else.

Talk with your teacher and classmates about how you might share these special pages that praise God for His Creation.

Correct Formation of Manuscript Letters and Numbers

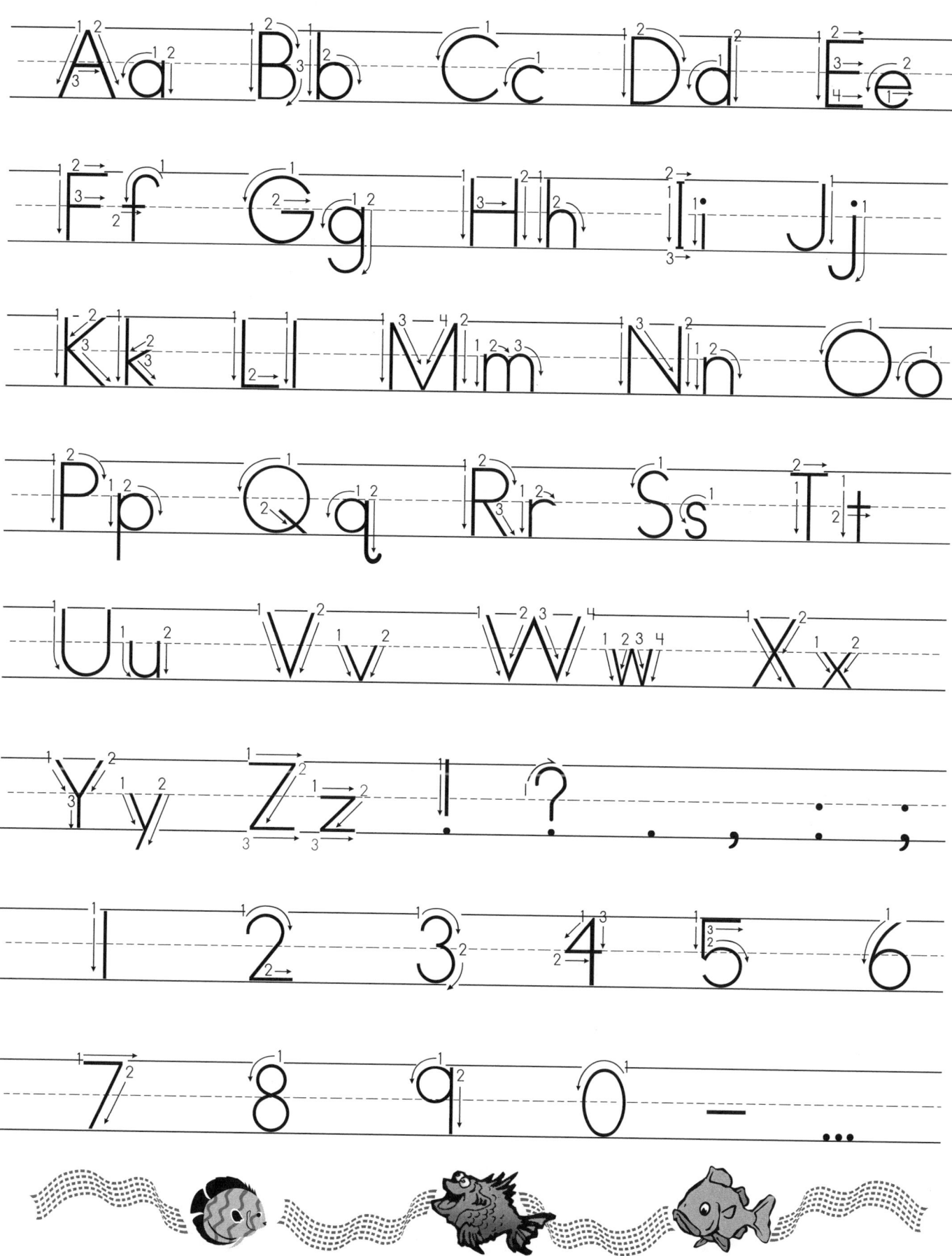

Correct Formation of Cursive Letters

Aa Bb Cc Dd

Ee Ff Gg Hh

Ii Jj Kk Ll

Mm Nn Oo Pp

Qq Rr Ss Tt

Uu Vv Ww Xx

Yy Zz

Introduction

Read the introductory message with the children and discuss what the year will hold.

Position pages:

Review the correct pencil, paper, hand and posture positions for good writing.

Special pages:

1. The theme for the quotes and verses for this year's program is: Praising God in His Creation. Each selection is meant to widen the child's awareness of the beauty and wonder of God's creation. Many selections are taken from the Bible (New International Version). Other quotes are taken from famous poets.

2. On the poetry quotations, you will find the full text of the poem printed in the Teacher's Guide. The portion to be written by the children is set in a larger type size for easy recognition.

3. Use the quote or verse each day in class throughout the week. Write it on the board or on poster board and place it in a prominent place so that the children become accustomed to seeing and reading it.

4. Introduce any unfamiliar or new words.

5. Pay careful attention to the practice page. Note reversals and any other formation or spacing problems that will cause difficulty when the child makes the final copy on the specially provided page.

6. Discuss with the children the ways in which they can share their special pages with others.

Manuscript letter and number formation guide.

1. Have a copy of the manuscript letter formation guide available for each child. Place either in a writing folder or collect and redistribute the guides each day.

2. Encourage children to check with the guide whenever they are unsure of the correct formation of a letter.

Cursive letter formation guide.

1. Have a copy of the cursive letter formation guide available for each child by the fifteenth week.

2. Encourage the children to check the guide frequently as they begin learning to write in cursive.

Lessons.

Lessons 1–75 are review and practice of manuscript letter formation, words and sentences.

Lessons 76–126 introduce the formation of the cursive alphabet and the formation of words and sentences using cursive writing.

Lessons 127–160 contain cursive practice with some manuscript review lessons.

If for some reason, a child is not ready to begin cursive writing at this time, alternate manuscript lessons are provided in this Teacher's Guide.

General guidelines for daily lessons:

1. Read and review the Bible verse or quote for the week each day.
2. Do some warm-up activities.
3. Check hand, pencil, paper and posture positions.
4. Review the letters and words to be written for the day.
5. Observe position, formation and spacing. Watch for letter reversals.
6. Urge children to work carefully to form each letter.
7. Let the children break the practice session if the lesson or quotation is long. Show them some simple hand shaking and movement exercises they can do if their hands become tired or cramped.
8. Praise all efforts.
9. Circle the best attempt for each letter and word.

Scope & Sequence

14

Lesson 1	Lines 1 & 2	a, b, c, d, e, f, g
	Lines 3 & 4	h, i, j, k, l, m, n
	Lines 5 & 6	o, p, q, r, s, t, u
	Lines 7 & 8	v, w, x, y, z, ., ,, :
	Lines 9 & 10	Blank lines for additional practice
Lesson 2	Lines 1 & 2	A, B, C, D, E, F, G
	Lines 3 & 4	H, I, J, K, L, M, N
	Lines 5 & 6	O, P, Q, R, S, T, U
	Lines 7 & 8	V, W, X, Y, Z
	Lines 9 & 10	Blank lines for additional practice
Lesson 3	Lines 1 & 2	earth
	Lines 3 & 4	everything
	Lines 5 & 6	world
	Lines 7 & 8	The earth is the Lord's
	Lines 9 & 10	Blank lines for additional practice
Lesson 4	Practice Psalm 24:1	
Lesson 5	Verse on Special Page	
Lesson 6	Lines 1 & 2	G, g
	Lines 3 & 4	T, t
	Lines 5 & 6	heavens
	Lines 7 & 8	skies
	Lines 9 & 10	Blank lines for additional practice
Lesson 7	Lines 1 & 2	proclaim
	Lines 3 & 4	declare
	Lines 5 & 6	work
	Lines 7 & 8	hands
	Lines 9 & 10	Blank lines for additional practice
Lesson 8	Lines 1 & 2	The heavens declare
	Lines 3 & 4	God's glory. The skies
	Lines 5 & 6	proclaim God's work.
	Lines 7 & 8	God's hand made all things.
	Lines 9 & 10	All things praise God.
Lesson 9	Practice Psalm 19:1	
Lesson 10	Verse on Special Page	

Lesson 11	Lines 1 & 2	S, s
	Lines 3 & 4	W, w
	Lines 5 & 6	1, 2, 3, 4, 5, 6, 7, 8, 9, 0
	Lines 7 & 8	moon
	Lines 9 & 10	Blank lines for additional practice
Lesson 12	Lines 1 & 2	flower.
	Lines 3 & 4	bower;
	Lines 5 & 6	delight,
	Lines 7 & 8	night.
	Lines 9 & 10	Blank lines for additional practice
Lesson 13	Lines 1 & 2	The moon with delight
	Lines 3 & 4	smiles on the night.
	Lines 5 & 6	The moon sits silent.
	Lines 7 & 8	It sits in the heavens.
	Lines 9 & 10	Blank lines for additional practice
Lesson 14	Practice Poem "Night"	
Lesson 15	Poem on Special Page	
Lesson 16	Lines 1 & 2	M, m
	Lines 3 & 4	A, a
	Lines 5 & 6	H, h
	Lines 7 & 8	R, r
	Lines 9 & 10	Blank lines for additional practice
Lesson 17	Lines 1 & 2	rainbow
	Lines 3 & 4	leaps up
	Lines 5 & 6	behold
	Lines 7 & 8	old
	Lines 9 & 10	Blank lines for additional practice
Lesson 18	Lines 1 & 2	When I see a rainbow,
	Lines 3 & 4	my heart leaps.
	Lines 5 & 6	William Wordsworth
	Lines 7 & 8	Behold, God's rainbow!
	Lines 9 & 10	Blank lines for additional practice
Lesson 19	Practice poem "My Heart Leaps Up"	
Lesson 20	Poem on Special Page	

Lesson 21	Lines 1 & 2	B, b
	Lines 3 & 4	C, c
	Lines 5 & 6	D, d
	Lines 7 & 8	between
	Lines 9 & 10	Blank lines for additional practice

Lesson 22	Lines 1 & 2	sign
	Lines 3 & 4	covenant
	Lines 5 & 6	earth
	Lines 7 & 8	clouds
	Lines 9 & 10	Blank lines for additional practice

Lesson 23	Lines 1 & 2	Genesis
	Lines 3 & 4	I will set my rainbow.
	Lines 5 & 6	It will be a sign.
	Lines 7 & 8	I make a covenant.
	Lines 9 & 10	Blank lines for additional practice

Lesson 24   Practice Genesis 9:13

Lesson 25   Verse on Special Page

Lesson 26	Lines 1 & 2	E, e
	Lines 3 & 4	F, f
	Lines 5 & 6	J, j
	Lines 7 & 8	K, k
	Lines 9 & 10	Blank lines for additional practice

Lesson 27	Lines 1 & 2	When
	Lines 3 & 4	ever
	Lines 5 & 6	Whenever
	Lines 7 & 8	brings
	Lines 9 & 10	Blank lines for additional practice

Lesson 28	Lines 1 & 2	appears
	Lines 3 & 4	remember
	Lines 5 & 6	living
	Lines 7 & 8	creatures
	Lines 9 & 10	Blank lines for additional practice

Lesson 29   Practice Genesis 9:14

Lesson 30   Verse on Special Page

Lesson 31	Lines 1 & 2	P, p
	Lines 3 & 4	L, l
	Lines 5 & 6	provides
	Lines 7 & 8	ravens
	Lines 9 & 10	Blank lines for additional practice

Lesson 32	Lines 1 & 2	cattle
	Lines 3 & 4	supplies
	Lines 5 & 6	covers
	Lines 7 & 8	young
	Lines 9 & 10	Blank lines for additional practice

Lesson 33	Lines 1 & 2	thanksgiving
	Lines 3 & 4	Sing to the Lord!
	Lines 5 & 6	He supplies the earth.
	Lines 7 & 8	He provides food.
	Lines 9 & 10	Blank lines for additional practice

| **Lesson 34** | Practice Psalm 147:7, 8-9 |

| **Lesson 35** | Verse on Special Page |

Lesson 36	Lines 1 & 2	Wh
	Lines 3 & 4	Who
	Lines 5 & 6	what
	Lines 7 & 8	where
	Lines 9 & 10	Blank lines for additional practice

Lesson 37	Lines 1 & 2	wind
	Lines 3 & 4	neither
	Lines 5 & 6	nor
	Lines 7 & 8	leaves
	Lines 9 & 10	trembling

Lesson 38	Lines 1 & 2	Have you seen the wind?
	Lines 3 & 4	Leaves tremble.
	Lines 5 & 6	The wind is passing by.
	Lines 7 & 8	The wind bends the trees.
	Lines 9 & 10	Blank lines for additional practice

| **Lesson 39** | Practice poem "Who Has Seen the Wind" |

| **Lesson 40** | Poem on Special Page |

Lesson 51	Lines 1 & 2	V, v
	Lines 3 & 4	X, x
	Lines 5 & 6	Y, y
	Lines 7 & 8	Z, z
	Lines 9 & 10	Blank lines for additional practice

Lesson 52	Lines 1 & 2	little ones
	Lines 3 & 4	baby ones
	Lines 5 & 6	shadows pass
	Lines 7 & 8	over grass
	Lines 9 & 10	Blank lines for additional practice

Lesson 53	Lines 1 & 2	clouds sail by
	Lines 3 & 4	over the sky
	Lines 5 & 6	Where am I?
	Lines 7 & 8	A. A. Milne
	Lines 9 & 10	Blank lines for additional practice

| **Lesson 54** | Practice poem "Spring Morning" |

| **Lesson 55** | Poem on Special Page |

Lesson 56	Lines 1 & 2	see
	Lines 3 & 4	spin
	Lines 5 & 6	Solomon
	Lines 7 & 8	splendor
	Lines 9 & 10	Blank lines for additional practice

Lesson 57	Lines 1 & 2	lily
	Lines 3 & 4	lilies
	Lines 5 & 6	dressed like one
	Lines 7 & 8	labor
	Lines 9 & 10	Blank lines for additional practice

Lesson 58	Lines 1 & 2	field
	Lines 3 & 4	they
	Lines 5 & 6	these
	Lines 7 & 8	They do not labor
	Lines 9 & 10	or spin.

| **Lesson 59** | Practice Matthew 6:28-29 |

| **Lesson 60** | Verse on Special Page |

Lesson 61	Lines 1 & 2	over
	Lines 3 & 4	o'er
	Lines 5 & 6	vale
	Lines 7 & 8	valley
	Lines 9 & 10	Blank lines for additional practice
Lesson 62	Lines 1 & 2	wandered
	Lines 3 & 4	crowd
	Lines 5 & 6	hills
	Lines 7 & 8	daffodils
	Lines 9 & 10	Blank lines for additional practice
Lesson 63	Lines 1 & 2	A cloud floats high.
	Lines 3 & 4	A host is a crowd.
	Lines 5 & 6	Daffodils are golden yellow.
	Lines 7 & 8	A vale is a valley.
	Lines 9 & 10	Blank lines for additional practice
Lesson 64	Practice poem "I Wandered Lonely as a Cloud"	
Lesson 65	Poem on Special Page	
Lesson 66	Lines 1 & 2	see tree
	Lines 3 & 4	red head
	Lines 5 & 6	fruit-laden
	Lines 7 & 8	cherry tree
	Lines 9 & 10	Blank lines for additional practice
Lesson 67	Lines 1 & 2	balls of shining red
	Lines 3 & 4	decking a leafy head
	Lines 5 & 6	Cherries are red.
	Lines 7 & 8	They are fair to see.
	Lines 9 & 10	Blank lines for additional practice
Lesson 68	Lines 1 & 2	Christina
	Lines 3 & 4	Rossetti
	Lines 5 & 6	Oh, Fair to See
	Lines 7 & 8	Blank lines for additional practice
	Lines 9 & 10	Blank lines for additional practice
Lesson 69	Practice poem "Oh, Fair to See"	
Lesson 70	Poem on Special Page	

Lesson 71   Lines 1 & 2   season
              Lines 3 & 4   singing
              Lines 5 & 6   cooing
              Lines 7 & 8   Song of Songs
              Lines 9 & 10   Blank lines for additional practice

Lesson 72   Lines 1 & 2   The winter is past.
              Lines 3 & 4   The rains are over.
              Lines 5 & 6   The rains are gone.
              Lines 7 & 8   Flowers appear.
              Lines 9 & 10   Blank lines for additional practice

Lesson 73   Lines 1 & 2   The season has come to
              Lines 3 & 4   sing. Doves coo
              Lines 5 & 6   in the land. We hear
              Lines 7 & 8   the doves cooing.
              Lines 9 & 10   We praise God!

Lesson 74   Practice Song of Songs 2:11-12

Lesson 75   Verse on Special Page

Lesson 76   Lines 1 & 2   A, $\mathcal{A}$
              Lines 3 & 4   a, a
              Lines 5 & 6 $\mathcal{A}$
              Lines 7 & 8 a
              Lines 9 & 10   The Lord is my Shepherd.

Alt. Less. 76 Lines 1 & 2   shepherd
                 Lines 3 & 4   pastures
                 Lines 5 & 6   quiet
                 Lines 7 & 8   The Lord is my Shepherd.
                 Lines 9 & 10   Blank lines for additional practice

Lesson 77   Lines 1 & 2   C, C
              Lines 3 & 4   c, c
              Lines 5 & 6 C
              Lines 7 & 8 c
              Lines 9 & 10 ca

Alt. Less. 77 Lines 1 & 2   I shall not want.
                 Lines 3 & 4   He leads me.
                 Lines 5 & 6   He restores my soul.
                 Lines 7 & 8   Blank lines for additional practice
                 Lines 9 & 10   Blank lines for additional practice

Lesson 78	Lines 1 & 2	O, *O*
	Lines 3 & 4	o, *o*
	Lines 5 & 6	*O*
	Lines 7 & 8	*o*
	Lines 9 & 10	*oa*

Alt. Less. 78	Lines 1 & 2	I lie down.
	Lines 3 & 4	I rest beside quiet waters.
	Lines 5 & 6	Blank lines for additional practice
	Lines 7 & 8	Blank lines for additional practice
	Lines 9 & 10	Blank lines for additional practice

Lesson 79   Practice Psalm 23:1-2

Lesson 80   Verse on Special Page

Lesson 81	Lines 1 & 2	D, *D*
	Lines 3 & 4	d, *d*
	Lines 5 & 6	*D*
	Lines 7 & 8	*d*
	Lines 9 & 10	*da*

Alt. Less. 81	Lines 1 & 2	anywhere
	Lines 3 & 4	blue-bells
	Lines 5 & 6	? ? ? ?
	Lines 7 & 8	Blank lines for additional practice
	Lines 9 & 10	Blank lines for additional practice

Lesson 82	Lines 1 & 2	Q, *Q*
	Lines 3 & 4	q, *q*
	Lines 5 & 6	*Q*
	Lines 7 & 8	*q*
	Lines 9 & 10	*cod*

Alt. Less. 82	Lines 1 & 2	Where am I going?
	Lines 3 & 4	Where are you going?
	Lines 5 & 6	What does it matter?
	Lines 7 & 8	Blank lines for additional practice
	Lines 9 & 10	Blank lines for additional practice

Lesson 83	Lines 1 & 2	G, *G*
	Lines 3 & 4	g, *g*
	Lines 5 & 6	*G*
	Lines 7 & 8	*g*
	Lines 9 & 10	*go*

Alt. Less. 101	Lines 1 & 2	withered leaves
	Lines 3 & 4	elder trees
	Lines 5 & 6	frosty air
	Lines 7 & 8	Blank lines for additional practice
	Lines 9 & 10	Blank lines for additional practice

Lesson 102	Lines 1 & 2	P, *P*
	Lines 3 & 4	p, *p*
	Lines 5 & 6	*P*
	Lines 7 & 8	*p*
	Line 9	*pat*
	Lines 10	*apple*

Alt. Less. 102	Lines 1 & 2	See the kitten
	Lines 3 & 4	sporting with leaves.
	Lines 5 & 6	through the calm and
	Lines 7 & 8	frosty air
	Lines 9 & 10	Blank lines for additional practice

Lesson 103	Lines 1 & 2	N, *n*
	Lines 3 & 4	n, *n*
	Lines 5 & 6	*n*
	Lines 7 & 8	*n*
	Lines 9 & 10	*kitten*

Alt. Less. 103	Lines 1 & 2	one, two, and three
	Lines 3 & 4	Of the morning bright
	Lines 5 & 6	and fair
	Lines 7 & 8	Blank lines for additional practice
	Lines 9 & 10	Blank lines for additional practice

Lesson 104   Practice poem "The Kitten and the Falling Leaves"

Lesson 105   Poem on Special Page

Lesson 106	Lines 1 & 2	M, *m*
	Lines 3 & 4	m, *m*
	Lines 5 & 6	*m*
	Lines 7 & 8	*m*
	Lines 9 & 10	*me*

Alt. Less. 106	Lines 1 & 2	Tiger ! Tiger !
	Lines 3 & 4	burning bright
	Lines 5 & 6	forests of the night
	Lines 7 & 8	Blank lines for additional practice
	Lines 9 & 10	Blank lines for additional practice

Lesson 107	Lines 1 & 2	R, *R*
	Lines 3 & 4	r, *r*
	Lines 5 & 6	*R*
	Lines 7 & 8	*r*
	Lines 9 & 10	*Tiger*

Alt. Less. 107	Lines 1 & 2	immortal hand
	Lines 3 & 4	fearful symmetry
	Lines 5 & 6	William Blake
	Lines 7 & 8	Blank lines for additional practice
	Lines 9 & 10	Blank lines for additional practice

Lesson 108	Lines 1 & 2	*fearful*
	Lines 3 & 4	*night*
	Lines 5 & 6	*bright*
	Lines 7 & 8	*hand*
	Lines 9 & 10	*could*

Alt. Less. 108	Lines 1 & 2	fearful
	Lines 3 & 4	night
	Lines 5 & 6	bright
	Lines 7 & 8	hand
	Lines 9 & 10	could

| **Lesson 109** | Practice poem "The Tiger" |

| **Lesson 110** | Poem on Special Page |

Lesson 111	Lines 1 & 2	U, *U*
	Lines 3 & 4	u, *u*
	Lines 5 & 6	*U*
	Lines 7 & 8	*u*
	Lines 9 & 10	*up* *cup*

Alt. Less. 111	Lines 1 & 2	crooked hands
	Lines 3 & 4	clasps the crag
	Lines 5 & 6	close to the sun
	Lines 7 & 8	Blank lines for additional practice
	Lines 9 & 10	Blank lines for additional practice

Lesson 112	Lines 1 & 2	S, *S*
	Lines 3 & 4	s, *s*
	Lines 5 & 6	*S*
	Lines 7 & 8	*s*
	Lines 9 & 10	*sun* *sea*

Alt. Less. 112	Lines 1 & 2	azure world
	Lines 3 & 4	wrinkled sea
	Lines 5 & 6	ringed the world
	Lines 7 & 8	Blank lines for additional practice
	Lines 9 & 10	Blank lines for additional practice
Lesson 113	Lines 1 & 2	W, *W*
	Lines 3 & 4	w, *w*
	Lines 5 & 6	*W*
	Lines 7 & 8	*w*
	Line 9	*with*
	Line 10	*world*
Alt. Less. 113	Lines 1 & 2	mountains walls,
	Lines 3 & 4	thunderbolt
	Lines 5 & 6	He watches and falls
	Lines 7 & 8	Blank lines for additional practice
	Lines 9 & 10	Blank lines for additional practice
Lesson 114	Practice poem "The Eagle"	
Lesson 115	Poem on Special Page	
Lesson 116	Lines 1 & 2	Y, *Y*
	Lines 3 & 4	y, *y*
	Lines 5 & 6	*Y*
	Lines 7 & 8	*y*
	Lines 9 & 10	*yes* *you*
Alt. Less. 116	Lines 1 & 2	A Bird Came Down the
	Lines 3 & 4	Walk
	Lines 5 & 6	Emily
	Lines 7 & 8	Dickinson
	Lines 9 & 10	Blank lines for additional practice
Lesson 117	Lines 1 & 2	V, *V*
	Lines 3 & 4	v, *v*
	Lines 5 & 6	*V*
	Lines 7 & 8	*v*
	Lines 9 & 10	*very*
Alt. Less. 117	Lines 1 & 2	halves
	Lines 3 & 4	fellow
	Lines 5 & 6	worm
	Lines 7 & 8	Blank lines for additional practice
	Lines 9 & 10	Blank lines for additional practice

Lesson 118   Lines 1 & 2   *A bird came down.*
                  Lines 3 & 4   *He did not know I*
                  Lines 5 & 6   *saw He bit a worm*
                  Lines 7 & 8   *in halves. He ate*
                  Lines 9 & 10   *the fellow, raw.*

Alt. Less. 118 Lines 1 & 2   A bird came down.
                    Lines 3 & 4   He did not know I saw
                    Lines 5 & 6   He bit a worm in halves.
                    Lines 7 & 8   He ate the fellow, raw.
                    Lines 9 & 10   Blank lines for additional practice

Lesson 119   Practice poem

Alt. Less. 119 **"A Bird Came Down the Walk"**

A bird came down the

walk;

He did not know I saw:

He bit an angle–worm

in halves

And ate the fellow, raw.

                            Emily Dickinson

Lesson 120   Poem on Special Page

Lesson 121   Lines 1 & 2   J, *J*
                  Lines 3 & 4   j, *j*
                  Lines 5 & 6   *J*
                  Lines 7 & 8   *j*
                  Line 9   *jump*
                  Line 10   *joy*

Alt. Less. 121 Lines 1 & 2   crowing
                    Lines 3 & 4   flowing
                    Lines 5 & 6   green field sleeps
                    Lines 7 & 8   written
                    Lines 9 & 10   Blank lines for additional practice

Lesson 122   Lines 1 & 2   X, *X*
                  Lines 3 & 4   x, *x*
                  Lines 5 & 6   *X*
                  Lines 7 & 8   *x*
                  Lines 9 & 10   *x-ray*   *ax*

30   *Horizons Penmanship Grade 2*

Alt. Less. 122	Lines 1 & 2	twitter
	Lines 3 & 4	glitter
	Lines 5 & 6	stream
	Lines 7 & 8	March
	Lines 9 & 10	Blank lines for additional practice
Lesson 123	Lines 1 & 2	*The cock is crowing.*
	Lines 3 & 4	*The stream is flowing.*
	Lines 5 & 6	*The small birds*
	Lines 7 & 8	*twitter. The lake doth*
	Lines 9 & 10	*glitter. The green field.*
	Lines 11 & 12	*sleep in the sun.*
Alt. Less. 123	Lines 1 & 2	The cock is crowing. The
	Lines 3 & 4	stream is flowing. The
	Lines 5 & 6	small birds twitter. The
	Lines 7 & 8	lake doth glitter. The green
	Lines 9 & 10	field sleeps in the sun.
Lesson 124	Practice poem	

Alt. Less. 124   **"Written in March"**

The cock is crowing,

Stream is flowing,

The small birds twitter,

The lake doth glitter,

The green field sleeps in

the sun

Lesson 125	Poem on Special Page	
Lesson 126	Lines 1 & 2	Z, *Z*
	Lines 3 & 4	z, *z*
	Lines 5 & 6	*Z*
	Lines 7 & 8	*z*
	Line 9	*zoo*
	Line 10	*zebra*
Alt. Less. 126	Lines 1 & 2	you'd
	Lines 3 & 4	that's
	Lines 5 & 6	! ! ! !
	Lines 7 & 8	Blank lines for additional practice
	Lines 9 & 10	Blank lines for additional practice

Lesson 127	Lines 1 & 2	*Aa, Bb, Cc, Dd, Ee*
	Lines 3 & 4	*Ff, Gg, Hh, Ii, Jj*
	Lines 5 & 6	*Kk, Ll, Mm, Nn, Oo*
	Lines 7 & 8	*Pp, Qq, Rr, Ss, Tt*
	Lines 9 & 10	*Uu, Vv, Ww, Xx, Yy, Zz*
Alt. Less. 127	Lines 1 & 2	A bird can fly.
	Lines 3 & 4	Can you fly?
	Lines 5 & 6	What do you want to
	Lines 7 & 8	do?
	Lines 9 & 10	Blank lines for additional practice
Lesson 128	Lines 1 & 2	*If I were a bird,*
	Lines 3 & 4	*and lived on high*
	Lines 5 & 6	*"That's where I*
	Lines 7 & 8	*wanted to go today!"*
	Lines 9 & 10	*A. A. Milne*
Alt. Less. 128	Lines 1 & 2	If I were a bird, and
	Lines 3 & 4	lived on high, and
	Lines 5 & 6	"That's where I wanted
	Lines 7 & 8	to go today!"
	Lines 9 & 10	A. A. Milne
Lesson 129	Practice poem "Spring Morning"	

Alt. Less. 129

If you were a bird, and
lived on high,
You'd lean on the wind
when the wind came by,
You'd say to the wind
when it took you away:
"That's where I wanted
to go today!"

A. A. Milne

Lesson 130	Poem on Special Page	
Lesson 131	Lines 1 & 2	*T There's*
	Lines 3 & 4	*S Small*
	Lines 5 & 6	*B Blue*
	Lines 7 & 8	*W Williams*
	Lines 9 & 10	*Blank lines for additional practice*

Alt. Less. 131	Lines 1 & 2	T T There's
	Lines 3 & 4	S S Small
	Lines 5 & 6	B B Blue
	Lines 7 & 8	W W William
	Lines 9 & 10	Blank lines for additional practice
Lesson 132	Lines 1 & 2	*mountains*
	Lines 3 & 4	*fountains*
	Lines 5 & 6	*sailing*
	Lines 7 & 8	*prevailing*
	Lines 9 & 10	*Blank lines for additional practice*
Alt. Less. 132	Lines 1 & 2	mountains
	Lines 3 & 4	fountains
	Lines 5 & 6	sailing
	Lines 7 & 8	prevailing
	Lines 9 & 10	Blank lines for additional practice
Lesson 133	Lines 1 & 2	*rain is over*
	Lines 3 & 4	*joy*
	Lines 5 & 6	*life*
	Lines 7 & 8	*Wordsworth*
	Lines 9 & 10	*Blank lines for additional practice*
Alt. Less. 133	Lines 1 & 2	rain is over
	Lines 3 & 4	joy
	Lines 5 & 6	life
	Lines 7 & 8	Wordsworth
	Lines 9 & 10	Blank lines for additional practice
Lesson 134	Practice poem "Written In March"	
Alt. Less. 134	There's joy in the mountains;	
	There's life in the fountains;	
	Small clouds are sailing,	
	Blue sky prevailing;	
	The rain is over and gone!	
	Wordsworth	

Lesson 135	Poem on Special Page	
Lesson 136	Lines 1 & 2	*L Lord*
	Lines 3 & 4	*G God*
	Lines 5 & 6	*P Psalm*
	Lines 7 & 8	*b born*
	Lines 9 & 10	*Blank lines for additional practice*
Alt. Less. 136	Lines 1 & 2	L L Lord
	Lines 3 & 4	G G God
	Lines 5 & 6	P P Psalm
	Lines 7 & 8	b b born
	Lines 9 & 10	Blank lines for additional practice
Lesson 137	Lines 1 & 2	*brought forth*
	Lines 3 & 4	*the earth*
	Lines 5 & 6	*the world*
	Lines 7 & 8	*everlasting*
	Lines 9 & 10	*Blank lines for additional practice*
Alt. Less. 137	Lines 1 & 2	brought forth
	Lines 3 & 4	the earth
	Lines 5 & 6	the world
	Lines 7 & 8	everlasting
	Lines 9 & 10	Blank lines for additional practice
Lesson 138	Lines 1 & 2	*You are God. You*
	Lines 3 & 4	*brought forth the*
	Lines 5 & 6	*earth. You brought*
	Lines 7 & 8	*forth the world.*
	Lines 9 & 10	*You are everlasting.*
Alt. Less. 138	Lines 1 & 2	You are God. You
	Lines 3 & 4	brought forth the
	Lines 5 & 6	earth. You brought
	Lines 7 & 8	forth the world.
	Lines 9 & 10	You are everlasting.
Lesson 139	Practice Psalm 90:2	
Alt. Less. 139	Lord,	
	Before the mountains	
	were born or you brought	
	forth the earth and the	
	world, from everlasting to	
	everlasting you are God.	

34

Horizons Penmanship Grade 2

Lesson 146   Lines 1 & 2   *A B C D E F G*
                 Lines 3 & 4   *H I J K L M N*
                 Lines 5 & 6   *O P Q R S T U*
                 Lines 7 & 8   *V W X Y Z*
                 Lines 9 & 10   *Blank lines for additional practice*

Alt. Less. 146   Lines 1 & 2   A B C D E F G
                      Lines 3 & 4   H I J K L M N
                      Lines 5 & 6   O P Q R S T U
                      Lines 7 & 8   V W X Y Z
                      Lines 9 & 10   Blank lines for additional practice

Lesson 147   Lines 1 & 2   *a b c d e f g*
                 Lines 3 & 4   *h i j k l m n*
                 Lines 5 & 6   *o p q r s t u*
                 Lines 7 & 8   *v w x y z*
                 Lines 9 & 10   *Blank lines for additional practice*

Alt. Less. 147   Lines 1 & 2   a b c d e f g
                      Lines 3 & 4   h i j k l m n
                      Lines 5 & 6   o p q r s t u
                      Lines 7 & 8   v w x y z
                      Lines 9 & 10   Blank lines for additional practice

Lesson 148   Lines 1 & 2   *rivers clap*
                 Lines 3 & 4   *mountains sing*
                 Lines 5 & 6   *Lord comes*
                 Lines 7 & 8   *to judge the earth.*
                 Lines 9 & 10   *Blank lines for additional practice*

Alt. Less. 148   Lines 1 & 2   rivers clap
                      Lines 3 & 4   mountains sing
                      Lines 5 & 6   Lord comes
                      Lines 7 & 8   to judge the earth
                      Lines 9 & 10   Blank lines for additional practice

Lesson 149   Practice Psalm 98:8-9

Alt. Less. 149   Let the rivers clap their
                      hands.
                      let the mountains sing
                      together for joy:
                      let them sing before the Lord,
                      for he comes to judge
                      the earth.

Lesson 150   Verse on Special Page

Lesson 151   Lines 1 & 2   Aa Bb Cc Dd Ee Ff Gg
                 Lines 3 & 4   Hh Ii Jj Kk Ll Mm Nn
                 Lines 5 & 6   Oo Pp Qq Rr Ss Tt Uu
                 Lines 7 & 8   Vv Ww Xx Yy Zz
                 Lines 9 & 10   Blank lines for additional practice

Lesson 152   Lines 1 & 2   (On this day, the child writes the entire manuscript
                 Lines 3 & 4   alphabet on his/her own. They may look at the
                 Lines 5 & 6   guide, but no dotted lines.)
                 Lines 7 & 8
                 Lines 9 & 10

Lesson 153   Lines 1 & 2   established
                 Lines 3 & 4   temple
                 Lines 5 & 6   chief
                 Lines 7 & 8   raised above the hills
                 Lines 9 & 10   Blank lines for additional practice

Lesson 154   Practice Isaiah 2:2

Lesson 155   Verse on Special Page

Lesson 156   Lines 1 & 2   Aa Bb Cc Dd Ee
                 Lines 3 & 4   Ff Gg Hh Ii Jj
                 Lines 5 & 6   Kk Ll Mm Nn Oo
                 Lines 7 & 8   Pp Qq Rr Ss Tt
                 Lines 9 & 10   Uu Vv Ww Xx Yy Zz

Alt. Less. 156   Lines 1 & 2   A a   B b   C c   D d   E e
                     Lines 3 & 4   F f   G g   H h   I i   J j   K k
                     Lines 5 & 6   L l   M m   N n   O o   P p
                     Lines 7 & 8   Q q   R r   S s   T t   U u
                     Lines 9 & 10   V v   W w   X x   Y y   Z z

Lesson 157   Lines 1 & 2   (On this day, the child writes the entire cursive
                 Lines 3 & 4   alphabet on his/her own.)
                 Lines 5 & 6
                 Lines 7 & 8
                 Lines 9 & 10

Lesson 158   Lines 1 & 2   *sanctuary*

Lines 3 & 4   *mighty heavens*

Lines 5 & 6   *everything that*

Lines 7 & 8   *has breath*

Lines 9 & 10   *Praise the Lord.*

Alt. Less. 158   Lines 1 & 2   Sanctuary

Lines 3 & 4   mighty heavens

Lines 5 & 6   everything that has

Lines 7 & 8   breath

Lines 9 & 10   Praise the Lord.

Lesson 159   Practice Psalm 150:1, 6

Alt. Less. 159   Praise God in his
sanctuary;
praise him in his mighty
heavens.

Let everything that
has breath

Praise the Lord.

Lesson 160   Verse on Special Page

Teacher Lessons

Lesson 1 - Review Lower Case Alphabet

Teaching Tips:

1. Introduce the verse for the week: **Psalm 24:1**. Throughout the week, read other verses from the Book of Psalm and discuss them. Have the verse for the week displayed where the children can see it.

2. Review lower case alphabet.

   a: One stroke – circle (beginning at 2 o'clock position) and half-line. Children DO NOT pick up their pencils to make the half-line, but make the circle then continue up to the dotted line and down again.

   b: One stroke – tall line starting at the top line and circle down, up and around.

   c: One stroke – three-quarter circle beginning at the 2 o'clock position and ending at 4 o'clock position.

   d: One stroke – three-quarter circle (looks like a small "c") and a tall line (up to the top line). Use a continuous stroke around, up to the top then down.

   e: One stroke – straight line, small **c**. Begin in the middle of the space between the dotted line and the bottom line. Go across and then up and around.

   f: Two strokes – begin at 1 o'clock below the top line: and go up, around and straight down to the bottom line, pick up pencil and make a short cross line on the dotted line.

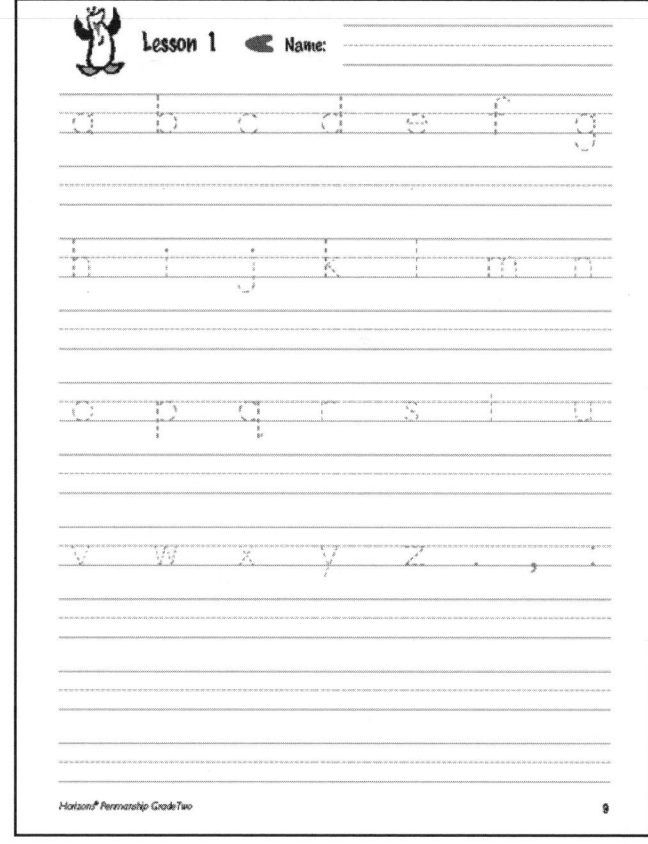

g: One stroke – small circle and hook. Begin about the 1 o'clock position, around, up, down below the bottom line, curve back up toward the bottom line (left side).

h: One stroke – tall line from top line to bottom line and arch. Start at top, line down, up, around and down.

i: Two strokes – half line and dot. Begin the first stroke on the dotted line, down to the bottom line. The second stroke is the dot in the middle of the space just above the dotted line.

j: Two strokes – begin at the dotted line and go down to the bottom line and continue below the line, then around and up toward the bottom line as in the small "g."

Pick up the pencil and make a dot in the middle of the space just above the the dotted line.

k: Two strokes – tall line beginning at the top line, two slanted lines into the tall one, beginning at the dotted line.

l: One stroke – from the top line to the bottom line.

m: One stroke – half-line and two arches beginning at the dotted line. Start at dotted line down, up, around, down, up, around and down again.

n: One stroke – half-line and arch beginning at the dotted line. Start at dotted line down, up, around and down.

o: One stroke – small circle. Begin at about the 2 o'clock position.

p: One stroke – line beginning at the dotted line and going down below the bottom line and small circle. Line down, up and around.

q: One stroke – small circle and hook. Begin about 1 o'clock position around, up, down below the bottom line, curve away. Note that the curve on this letter does not go up as high as the curve on the "g."

r: One stroke – half-line and small curve. Line down from dotted line, up and just around to about the 1 o'clock position.

s: One stroke – that curves its way between the dotted and bottom lines. Start at about the 1 o'clock position, curve to the dotted line up and around, down and around the bottom line.

t: Two strokes – a line beginning in the middle between the top line and the dotted line and going down and around the bottom line and a small line crossing it at the dotted line.

u: One stroke – start at dotted line down, around, up and down.

v: Two slanted strokes – each beginning at the dotted line and meeting at the bottom.

w: Four slanted stokes – each beginning at the dotted line and meeting at the bottom.

x: Two slanted strokes – each beginning at the dotted line and crossing in the middle of the the space between the dotted and bottom line.

y: Two slanted strokes – each beginning at the dotted line, the first stopping at the bottom line, the second extending down below the bottom line.

z: One stroke – between the dotted and bottom lines. Start across the dotted line, slant line back down to the bottom line, across the bottom.

3. Line 1: Trace the letters.
    Line 2: Write the letters from line 1.
    Line 3: Trace the letters.
    Line 4: Write the letters from line 3.
    Line 5: Trace the letters.
    Line 6: Write the letters from line 5.
    Line 7: Trace the letters and punctuation.
    Line 8: Write the letters and punctuation from line 7.
    Lines 9 & 10: Additional practice.

42

4. Correct any reversals or formation problems.

5. Watch formation and spacing.

6. Use the two blank lines at the bottom of the page to practice letters that need work.

7. Have the student(s) write their first name on the top line.

Bible Verse Lessons 1-5

"The earth is the Lord's, and everything in it, the world, and all who live in it."

(Psalm 24:1)

Lesson 2 - Review Capital Letters

Teaching Tips:

1. Read **Psalm 24:1**.

2. Review capital letters.

   A: Three strokes – two tall, slanted lines meeting at the top line; a short line across the dotted line to join the two slanted lines.

   B: Two strokes – tall line down and double loop (upper loop is slightly larger than the bottom loop).

   C: One stroke – start between one and 2 o'clock, up, around and stops between four and 5 o'clock.

   D: Two strokes – tall line down and large half circle.

   E: Four strokes – one tall line, three short lines out from the tall line, top line across, dotted line across, bottom line across.

   F: Three strokes – one tall line, two short lines out from the tall line, top line across, dotted line across.

   G: Two strokes – begins between one and 2 o'clock, up, around and stops at the dotted line. Pick up pencil and draw line across from the middle out to complete the letter.

   H: Three strokes – two tall lines separated (goal posts), one line across the dotted line to join the two tall lines.

   I: Three strokes – one tall line, two short lines, one across the top, one across the bottom.

   J: One stroke – beginning at the top line, straight down and around the bottom line.

   K: Two strokes – one tall line, two slanted lines (top into the middle of the tall line, then back out to the bottom line).

   L: One stroke – one tall line moving into a short line out from the bottom.

   M: Four strokes – two tall lines separated (like goal posts), two tall slanted lines – one from the top of each tall line down to the bottom line (meeting in the middle).

   N: Three strokes – two tall lines separated (goal posts) not quite as far apart as the "M"), one slanted tall line from the top of the first tall line to the bottom of the second tall line.

Horizons Penmanship Grade 2

O: One stroke – large circle, begins at 2 o'clock, up, around and back up.

P: Two strokes – tall line down and small loop at top between the top and dotted lines. Note that the top of the "P" is slightly wider than a half circle.

Q: Two strokes – large circle, slant line beginning in the middle of the space between the dotted and bottom lines and crossing the circle between the five and 6 o'clock position.

R: Two strokes – tall line down and combination of half loop between the top and dotted lines and slant line out to the bottom line (like a "P" with a cane).

S: One stroke – that curves its way between the top and bottom lines. Start at about the 1 o'clock position, curve to the top line up and around, down and around the bottom line.

T: Two strokes – one tall line, one short line across the top.

U: One stroke – begin as tall line, down, around and back up to the top line.

V: Two slanted strokes, each beginning at the top line and meeting at the bottom. Watch the slant.

W: Four slanted stokes – each beginning at the top line.

X: Two slanted strokes – each beginning at the top line and crossing on the dotted line.

Y: Three strokes – two slanted lines beginning at the top line and coming in to meet at the dotted line; a half-line straight down from the meeting point to the bottom line.

Z: One stroke – between the top and bottom lines. Start across the top line, slant line back down to the bottom line, across the bottom.

3. Line 1: Trace the letters.
   Line 2: Write the letters from line 1.
   Line 3: Trace the letters.
   Line 4: Write the letters from line 3.
   Line 5: Trace the letters.
   Line 6: Write the letters from line 5.
   Line 7: Trace the letters and punctuation.
   Line 8: Write the letters and punctuation from line 7.
   Lines 9 & 10: Additional practice.

4. Correct any reversals or formation problems.

5. Watch formation and spacing.

6. Use the two blank lines at the bottom of the page to practice letters that need work.

Bible Verse Lessons 1-5

"The earth is the Lord's, and everything in it, the world, and all who live in it."
(Psalm 24:1)

Lesson 3 - Practice Words

Teaching Tips:

1. Read **Psalm 24:1**.

2. Read the words and the sentence the children will write.

3. Stress that proper nouns like "Lord's" and the names of people begin with capital letters.

4. Review sequence of letters and new words.

5. Line 1: Trace the word and write the word as many times as it will fit on the line. Observe proper spacing.

   Line 2: Write the words as in line 1.

   Line 3: Trace the word and write the word as many times as it will fit on the line. Observe proper spacing.

   Line 4: Write the words as in line 3.

   Line 5: Trace the word and write the word as many times as it will fit on the line. Observe proper spacing.

   Line 6: Write the words as in line 5.

   Line 7: Trace the sentence.

   Line 8: Write the sentence from line 7.

   Lines 9 & 10: Additional practice.

6. Use the two blank lines at the bottom of the page to practice words that need work or to write original sentences.

Lesson 4 - Practice Bible Verse

Teaching Tips:

1. Review **Psalm 24:1** with the children.
2. Discuss the meaning of verse and reading of the citation or Scripture reference.
3. Trace the verse for the week.
4. Practice writing the verse for the week on a separate sheet of paper.
5. Remind them to write their first name on the top line.

Bible Verse Lessons 1-5

"The earth is the Lord's, and everything in it, the world, and all who live in it."

(Psalm 24:1)

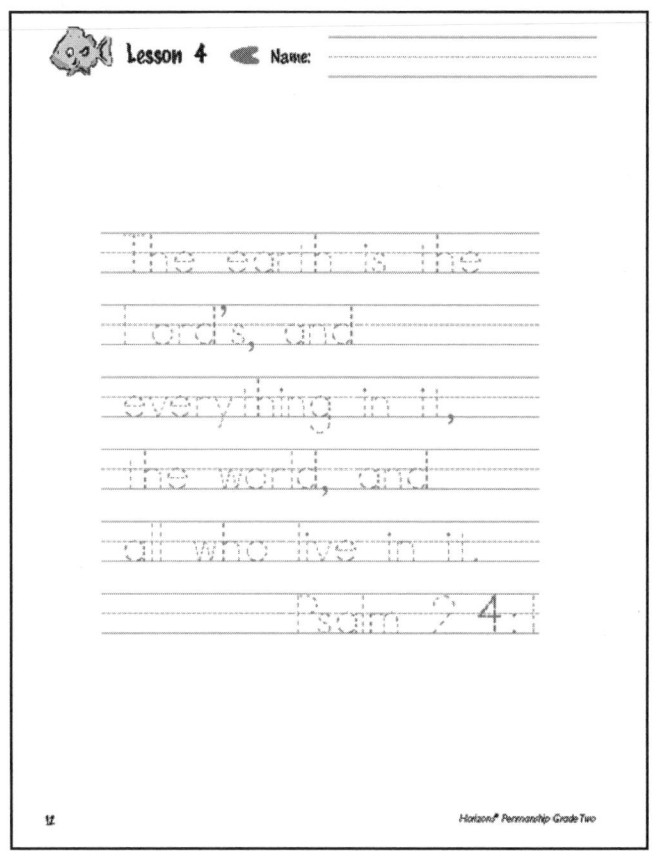

Lesson 5 - Special Page

Teaching Tips:

1. Explain that the children will copy the verse from Lesson 4 onto this special page using their best handwriting skills.
2. Allow the children to practice on the corresponding reproducible practice page from the back of this manual.
3. Complete the page.
4. Decide how this special page will be used.
5. Remind them to write their first name on the top line.

Lesson 6 - Letters
G, g, T, t

Teaching Tips:

1. Talk about the name and the sounds each letter makes. Note how each letter is formed.

2. Warm up for each letter and check position.

3. Trace and copy the letters while the teacher observes the position, formation and spacing.

4. Line 1: Trace the letters and complete the row with the same letter.

    Line 2: Write the letters from line 1.

    Line 3: Trace the letters and complete the row with the same letter.

    Line 4: Write the letters from line 3.

    Line 5.Trace the word and complete the row of the same word

    Line 6: Write the words from line 5.

    Line 7: Trace the word and complete the row of the same word

    Line 8: Write the words from line 7.

    Lines 9 & 10: Additional practice

5. Additional blank lines may be used for practice, for original sentences, for class sentences, for phrases, for rhyming words and so on.

6. Read: **Psalm 19:1**.

7. Throughout the week read other verses from the Psalm and discuss those which deal with the wonders of God's creation.

8. Remind them to write their first name on the top line.

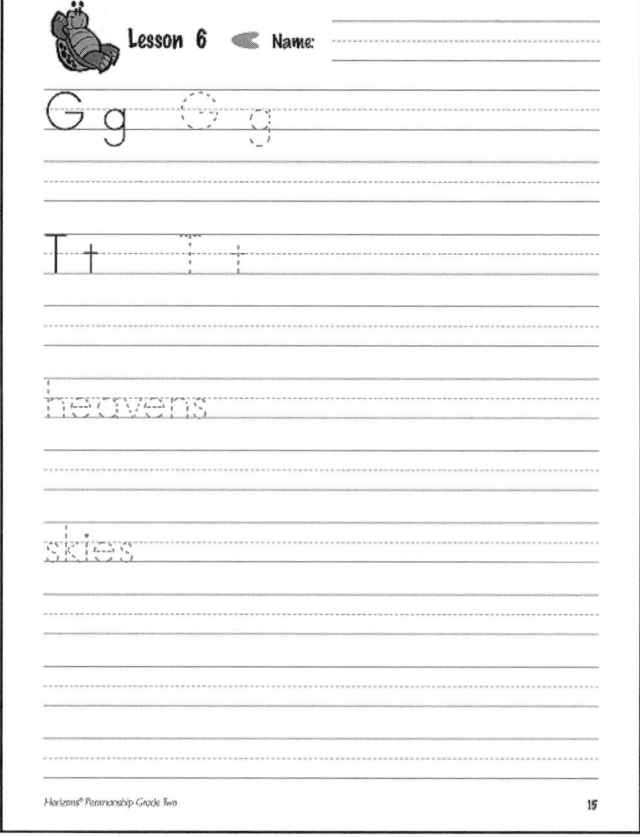

Bible Verse Lessons 6-10

"The heavens declare the glory of God; the skies proclaim the work of his hands." (Psalm 19:1)

Lesson 7 - Practice Words

Teaching Tips:

1. Help the children with these words. Have them trace the word then practice writing it to complete the line and the line below each word.

2. Watch formation and spacing.

3. Additional blank lines may be used for practice, for original sentences, for class sentences, for phrases, for rhyming words and so on.

4. Read: **Psalm 19:1**.

5. Throughout the week read other verses from the Book of Psalm and discuss those which deal with the wonders of God's creation.

Bible Verse Lessons 6-10

"The heavens declare the glory of God; the skies proclaim the work of his hands."

(Psalm 19:1)

Lesson 8 - Sentence Review

Teaching Tips:

1. Review sequence of letters and new words.

2. Help the children with these words. Have them trace the words then practice writing them on the blank lines.

3. Watch formation and spacing.

4. Read: **Psalm 19:1**.

5. Throughout the week read other verses from the Book of Psalm and discuss those which deal with the wonders of God's creation.

Lesson 7   Name:

proclaim

declare

work

hands

16   Horizons® Penmanship Grade Two

Lesson 8   Name:

the heavens declare

God's glory The skies

proclaim God's work.

God's hand made all things

All things praise God.

Horizons® Penmanship Grade Two   17

Lesson 9 - Practice Bible Verse

Teaching Tips:

1. Review **Psalm 19:1** with the children.

2. Discuss the meaning of verse and reading of the citation or Scripture reference.

3. Trace the verse for the week.

4. Practice writing the Psalm quote for the week on a separate sheet of paper.

5. Remind them to write their first name on the top line.

Bible Verse Lessons 6-10

"The heavens declare the glory of God; the skies proclaim the work of his hands."
(Psalm 19:1)

Lesson 10 - Special Page

Teaching Tips:

1. Explain that the children will copy the verse from Lesson 9 onto this special page using their best handwriting skills.

2. Allow the children to practice on the corresponding reproducible practice page from the back of this manual.

3. Complete the page.

4. Decide how this special page will be used.

5. Remind them to write their first name on the top line.

Lesson 9   Name: _____

The heavens declare the glory of God; the skies proclaim the work of his hands. Psalm 19:1

18   *Horizons® Penmanship Grade Two*

Lesson 10   Name: _____

Horizons® Penmanship Grade Two   19

Lesson 11 - Letters
S, s, W, w, 0-9

Teaching Tips:

1. Talk about the name and the sounds each letter makes. Note how each letter is formed.

2. Warm up for each letter and check position.

3. Trace and copy the letters and numbers while the teacher observes the position, formation and spacing.

   1: One stroke – tall line, from top line to bottom line.

   2: One stroke – around, down to the bottom line and across. Begin about the 11 o'clock position.

   3: One stroke – around and around. Begin about the 11 o'clock position and end at the 8 o'clock position.

   4: Two strokes – a slanted line down and across, tall line down.

   5: Two strokes – down and around, across the top.

   6: One stroke – start at the top line, curve down to the bottom line then around and up to the dotted line.

   7: One stroke – across the top line and slant down and back to the bottom line.

   8: One stroke – begins very much like an "S" then back around.

   9: One stroke – begins like a small circle between the top and dotted line at the 1 o'clock position, then straight line up and down to the bottom line.

S s   S   s

W w   W   w

1 2 3 4 5 6 7 8 9 0

moon

Horizons® Penmanship Grade Two

21

   0: One stroke – large oval. Note that the zero is slightly thinner than a capital "O."

4. Additional blank lines may be used for practice, for original sentences, for class sentences, for phrases, for rhyming words and so on.

5. Quote for the week: from *Night* by William Blake. (Selection in larger print.)

Night

The sun descending in the west.
The evening star does shine.
The birds are silent in their nest,
And I must seek for mine,
The moon like a flower,
In heavens high bower;
With silent delight,
Sits and smiles on the night.

Farewell green fields and happy groves,
Where flocks have took delight;
Where lambs have nibbled, silent moves
The feet of angels bright;
Unseen they pour blessing,
And joy without ceasing,
On each bud and blossom,
And each sleeping bosom.

They look in every thoughtless nest,
Where birds are covered warm;
They visit caves of every beast,
To keep them all from harm;
If they see any weeping,
That should have been sleeping
They pour sleep on their head
And sit down by their bed.

6. Through the week read selections from the entire poem to give the children the context for the poem.

7. Introduce words that may be unfamiliar, such as "bower."

8. Remind them to write their first name on the top line.

Lesson 12 - Practice Words

Teaching Tips:

1. Help the children with these words. Have them trace the word then practice writing it to complete the line and the line below each word.
2. Watch formation and spacing.
3. Additional blank lines may be used for practice, for original sentences, for class sentences, for phrases, for rhyming words and so on.
4. Review the quote for the week.

Poem for Lessons 11-15

"The moon like a flower, In heaven's high bower; With silent delight, Sits and smiles on the night."

Lesson 13 - Sentence Review

Teaching Tips:

1. Review sequences of letters and new words.
2. Help the children with these words. Have them trace the words then practice writing them on the blank lines.
3. Watch formation and spacing.
4. Review the quote.
5. Remind them to write their first name on the top line.

Lesson 14 - Practice Poem

Teaching Tips:

1. Review the quote from William Blake's poem the **Night** with the children.
2. Discuss the meaning of this poem and the section that the children are to practice.
3. Trace the quote for the week.
4. Practice writing the quote for the week on a separate sheet of paper.

Poem for Lessons 11-15

"The moon like a flower, In heaven's high bower; With silent delight, Sits and smiles on the night."

Lesson 15 - Special Page

Teaching Tips:

1. Explain that the children will copy the poem from Lesson 14 onto this special page using their best handwriting skills.
2. Allow the children to practice on the corresponding reproducible practice page from the back of this manual.
3. Complete the page.
4. Decide how this special page will be used.
5. Remind them to write their first name on the top line.

54

Lesson 16 - Letters M, m, A, a, H, h, R, r

Teaching Tips:

1. Talk about the name and the sounds each letter makes. Note how each letter is formed.

2. Warm up for each letter and check position.

3. Trace and copy the letters while the teacher observes the position, formation and spacing. Complete the line and the line below each of the letters.

4. Additional blank lines may be used for practice, for original sentences, for class sentences, for phrases, for rhyming words and so on.

5. Quote for the week: from *My Heart Leaps Up* by William Wordsworth.

My Heart Leaps Up

My heart leaps up when I behold
A rainbow in the sky:
So was it when my life began;
So is it now I am a man;
So be it when I shall grow old,
Or let me die!
The Child is father of the Man;
I could wish my days to be
Bound each to each by natural piety.

6. During the week read the entire poem.

7. Introduce author's name.

Mm   Mm

Aa   Aa

Hh   Hh

Rr   Rr

Horizons® Penmanship Grade Two   17

Lesson 17 - Practice Words

Teaching Tips:

1. Help the children with these words. Have them trace the word then practice writing it to complete the line end the line below it.

2. Watch formation and spacing.

3. Additional blank lines may be used for practice, for original sentences, for class sentences, for phrases, for rhyming words and so on.

4. Read the entire poem.

Poem for Lessons 16-20

"My heart leaps up when I behold A rainbow in the sky; So was it when my life began; So is it now I am a man; So be it when I shall grow old."

Lesson 18 - Sentence Review and Capitals

Teaching Tips:

1. Review sequence of letters and new words.

2. Help the children with these words. Have them trace the words then practice writing them.

3. Watch formation and spacing.

4. Stress that proper nouns like "God" and the names of people begin with capital letters.

5. Read the entire poem.

rainbow

leaps up

behold

old

When I see a rainbow,

my heart leaps.

William Wordsworth

Behold, God's rainbow

Lesson 19 - Practice Poem

Teaching Tips:

1. Review the quote from William Wordsworth's poem **My Heart Leaps Up** with the children.

2. Discuss the meaning of this poem and the section that the children are to practice.

3. Trace the poem.

4. Practice writing the quote for the week on a separate sheet of paper.

5. Remind them to write their first name on the top line.

Poem for Lessons 16-20

"My heart leaps up when I behold A rainbow in the sky; So was it when my life began; So is it now I am a man; So be it when I shall grow old."

Lesson 20 - Special Page

Teaching Tips:

1. Explain that the children will copy the poem from Lesson 19 onto this special page using their best handwriting skills.

2. Allow the children to practice on the corresponding reproducible practice page from the back of this manual.

3. Complete the page.

4. Decide how this special page will be used.

5. Remind them to write their first name on the top line.

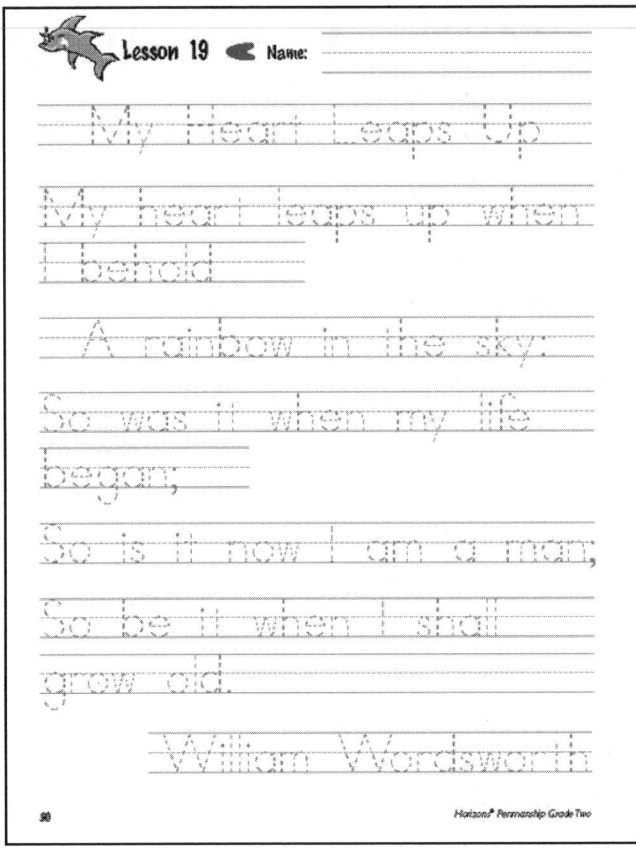

Lesson 21 - Letters B, b, C, c, D, d

Teaching Tips:

1. Introduce the verse for the week: **Genesis 9:13**. Throughout the week, read other verses from Genesis and discuss them. Have the verse for the week displayed where the children can see it.

2. Warm up for each letter and check position.

3. Trace and copy the letters while the teacher observes the position, formation and spacing. Complete the line and the line below each of the letters and words.

4. During the week read the story of Noah and discuss God's covenant (promise).

5. Introduce words that may be unfamiliar, such as "covenant."

6. Additional blank lines may be used for practice, for original sentences, for class sentences, for phrases, for rhyming words and so on.

7. The additional blank lines may be used for writing practice of the student(s) last name.

Bible Verse Lessons 21-25

"I have set my rainbow in the clouds, and it will be the sign of the covenant between me and the earth."

(Genesis 9:13)

Lesson 21 — Name:

B b   B b

C c   C c

D d   D d

between

Horizons® Penmanship Grade Two   35

Lesson 22 - Practice Words

Teaching Tips:

1. Help the children with these words. Have them trace the word then practice writing it.
2. Watch formation and spacing.
3. Continue reading the story of Noah and the discussion of God's Covenant.
4. Additional blank lines may be used for practice, for original sentences, for class sentences, for phrases, for rhyming words, for last name practice and so on.

Bible Verse Lessons 21-25

"I have set my rainbow in the clouds, and it will be the sign of the covenant between me and the earth."

(Genesis 9:13)

Lesson 23 - Sentence Review

Teaching Tips:

1. Review **Genesis 9:13**.
2. Review sequence of letters and new words.
3. Help the children with these words. Have them trace the words then practice writing them.
4. Watch formation and spacing.
5. Remind them to write their first name on the top line.

sign

covenant

earth

clouds

Genesis

I will set my rainbow.

It will be a sign.

I make a covenant.

Lesson 24 - Practice Bible Verse

Teaching Tips:

1. Review **Genesis 9:13** with the children.
2. Discuss the meaning of this verse that the children are to practice.
3. Trace the verse.
4. Practice writing the verse for the week on a separate sheet of paper.

Bible Verse Lessons 21-25

"I have set my rainbow in the clouds, and it will be the sign of the covenant between me and the earth."

(Genesis 9:13)

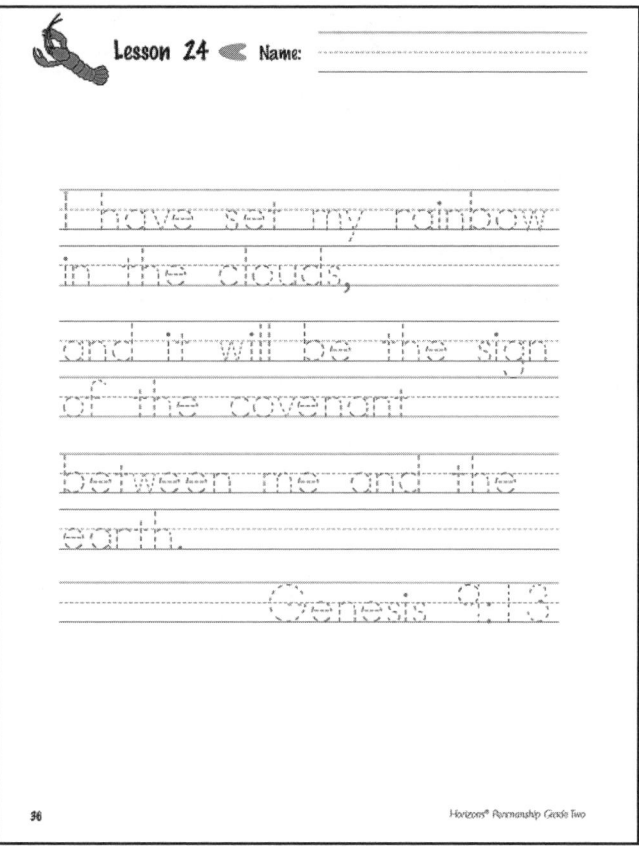

Lesson 25 - Special Page

Teaching Tips:

1. Explain that the children will copy the verse from Lesson 24 onto this special page using their best handwriting skills.
2. Allow the children to practice on the corresponding reproducible practice page from the back of this manual.
3. Complete the page.
4. Decide how this special page will be used.

Lesson 26 - Letters E, e, F, f, J, j, K, k

Teaching Tips:

1. Introduce the verse for the week: **Genesis 9:14**. Throughout the week, read other verses from Genesis and discuss them. Have the verse for the week displayed where the children can see it.

2. Warm up for each letter and check position.

3. Trace and copy the letters while the teacher observes the position, formation and spacing.

4. Review the story of Noah and God's rainbow.

5. Introduce new words: "whenever," "creatures."

6. Additional blank lines may be used for practice, for original sentences, for class sentences, for phrases, for rhyming words, for last name practice and so on.

Bible Verse Lessons 26-30

"Whenever I bring clouds over the earth and the rainbow appears in the clouds, I will remember my covenant between me and you and all living creatures."
(Genesis 9:14)

Lesson 26 Name:

E e

F f

J j

K k

Horizons® Penmanship Grade Two

39

Lesson 27 - Practice Words

Teaching Tips:

1. Help the children with these words. Have them trace the word then practice writing it to complete the line and the line below it.
2. Watch formation and spacing.
3. Additional blank lines may be used for practice, for original sentences, for class sentences, for phrases, for rhyming words, for last name practice and so on.

Bible Verse Lessons 26-30

"Whenever I bring clouds over the earth and the rainbow appears in the clouds, I will remember my covenant between me and you and all living creatures."

(Genesis 9:14)

Lesson 28 - Practice Words

Teaching Tips:

1. Help the children with these words. Have them trace the word then practice writing it to complete the line and the line below it.
2. Watch formation and spacing.
3. Additional blank lines may be used for practice, for original sentences, for class sentences, for phrases, for rhyming words, for last name practice and so on.

When
over
Whenever
brings

Horizons® Penmanship Grade Two

appears
remember
living
creatures

Horizons® Penmanship Grade Two

Lesson 29 - Practice Bible Verse

Teaching Tips:

1. Review **Genesis 9:14** with the children.
2. Discuss the meaning of this verse that the children are to practice.
3. Trace the verse.
4. Practice writing the verse for the week on a separate sheet of paper.

Bible Verse Lessons 26-30

"Whenever I bring clouds over the earth and the rainbow appears in the clouds, I will remember my covenant between me and you and all living creatures."
(Genesis 9:14)

Lesson 30 - Special Page

Teaching Tips:

1. Explain that the children will copy the verse from Lesson 29 onto this special page using their best handwriting skills.
2. Allow the children to practice on the corresponding reproducible practice page from the back of this manual.
3. Complete the page.
4. Decide how this special page will be used.

Lesson 31 - Letters
P, p, L, l

Teaching Tips:

1. Introduce the verse for the week: **Psalm 147:7, 8-9**. Throughout the week, read other verses from the Book of Psalms and discuss them. Have the verse for the week displayed where the children can see it.

2. Warm up for each letter and check position.

3. Trace and copy the letters while the teacher observes the position, formation and spacing.

4. Introduce new words: "Thanksgiving," "supplies," provides," "ravens."

5. Additional blank lines may be used for practice, for original sentences, for class sentences, for phrases, for rhyming words, for last name practice and so on.

Bible Verse Lessons 31-35

"Sing to the Lord with Thanksgiving; …
He covers the sky with clouds; he supplies the earth with rain and makes grass grow on the hills. He provides food for the cattle and for the young ravens when they call."
(Psalm 147:7, 8-9)

P p   P p

L l   L l

provides

ravens

Lesson 32 - Practice Words

Teaching Tips:

1. Help the children with these words. Have them trace the word then practice writing it.
2. Watch formation and spacing.
3. Additional blank lines may be used for practice, for original sentences, for class sentences, for phrases, for rhyming words, for last name practice and so on.

Bible Verse Lessons 31-35

"Sing to the Lord with Thanksgiving; …
He covers the sky with clouds; he supplies the earth with rain and makes grass grow on the hills. He provides food for the cattle and for the young ravens when they call."

(Psalm 147:7, 8-9)

Lesson 33 - Practice Word & Sentences

Teaching Tips:

1. Help the children with these words. Have them trace the word then practice writing it.
2. Review sequence of letters and new words.
3. Watch formation and spacing.
4. Stress that proper nouns like "Lord" and the names of people begin with capital letters.
5. Additional blank lines may be used for practice, for original sentences, for class sentences, for phrases, for rhyming words, for last name practice and so on.

Lesson 32   Name:

cattle

supplies

covers

young

46   Horizons Penmanship Grade Two

Lesson 33   Name:

thanksgiving

Sing to the Lord!

He supplies the earth.

He provides food.

Horizons Penmanship Grade Two   47

Lesson 34 - Practice Bible Verse

Teaching Tips:

1. Review **Psalm 147:7, 8-9** with the children.

2. Discuss the meaning of these verses that the children are to practice.

3. Discuss the purpose of the elipse. It is used when words or sentences are left out of a verse or quote.

4. Trace the verse.

5. Practice writing the verse for the week on a separate sheet of paper.

6. Allow extra time for practicing these verses because of the length.

Bible Verse Lessons 31-35

"Sing to the Lord with Thanksgiving; …
He covers the sky with clouds; he supplies the earth with rain and makes grass grow on the hills. He provides food for the cattle and for the young ravens when they call."
(Psalm 147:7, 8-9)

Lesson 35 - Special Page

Teaching Tips:

1. Explain that the children will copy the verse from Lesson 34 onto this special page using their best handwriting skills.

2. Allow the children to practice on the corresponding reproducible practice page from the back of this manual.

3. Allow extra time for copying these verses because of the length.

4. Complete the page.

5. Decide how this special page will be used.

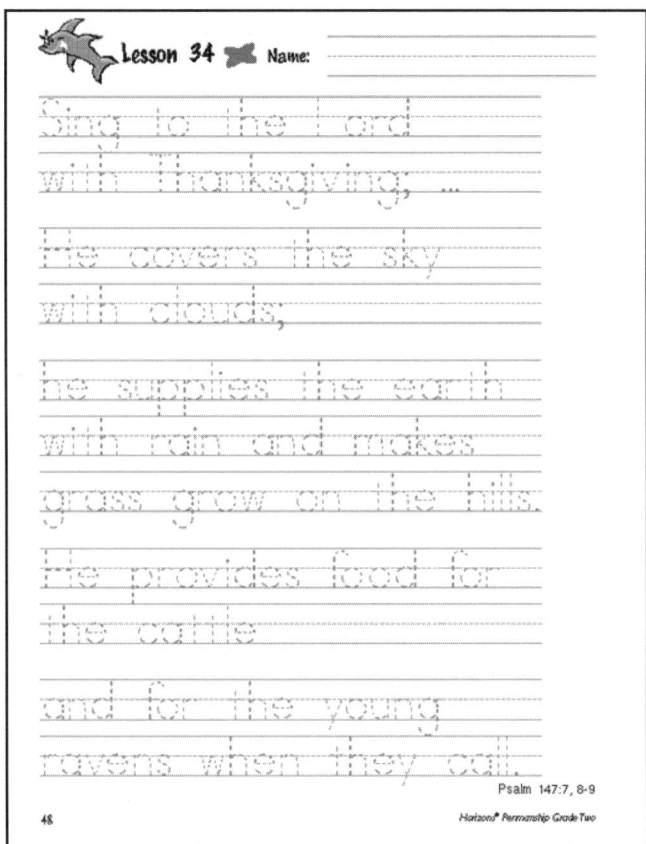

Lesson 36 - Practice Wh

Teaching Tips:

1. Talk about the sound these two letters make together. Note how each letter is formed.

2. Warm up for these letters and check position.

3. Trace and copy the letters while the teacher observes the position, formation and spacing.

4. Practice writing the words that start with these letters.

5. Additional blank lines may be used for practice, for original sentences, for class sentences, for phrases, for rhyming words and so on.

6. Quote for the week: from *Who Has Seen the Wind* by Christina Rossetti.

Who Has Seen the Wind?
Who has seen the wind?
Neither I nor you;
But when the leaves hang trembling
The wind is passing thro'.

7. During the week read the entire poem.

8. Introduce new words: "trembling," "thro'."

9. Introduce author's name.

Lesson 36 ◀ Name: _____

Wh   Wh

Who

what

where

Horizons® Penmanship Grade Two

51

Starfall.com
poetry
Who has seen the Wind
Poem w/ all verses

Lesson 37 - Practice Words

Teaching Tips:

1. Help the children with these words. Have them trace the word then practice writing it.
2. Watch formation and spacing.
3. During the week read the entire poem.
4. Additional blank lines may be used for practice, for original sentences, for class sentences, for phrases, for rhyming words and so on.

Poem for Lessons 36-40

"Who has seen the wind? Neither I nor you; But when the leaves hang trembling The wind is passing thro'."

Lesson 38 - Practice Sentences

Teaching Tips:

1. Help the children with these words. Have them trace the words then practice writing them.
2. Review sequence of letters and new words.
3. Watch formation and spacing.
4. During the week read the entire poem.
5. Additional blank lines may be used for practice, for original sentences, for class sentences, for phrases, for rhyming words and so on.

wind

neither

nor

leaves

trembling

Have you seen the wind?

Leaves tremble.

The wind is passing by.

The wind bends the trees.

Lesson 39 - Practice Poem

Teaching Tips:

1. Review the quote from Christina Rossetti's poem **Who Has Seen the Wind** with the children.
2. Discuss the meaning of this poem and the section that the children are to practice.
3. Trace the quote.
4. Practice writing the quote for the week on a separate sheet of paper.

Poem for Lessons 36-40

"Who has seen the wind? Neither I nor you; But when the leaves hang trembling The wind is passing thro'."

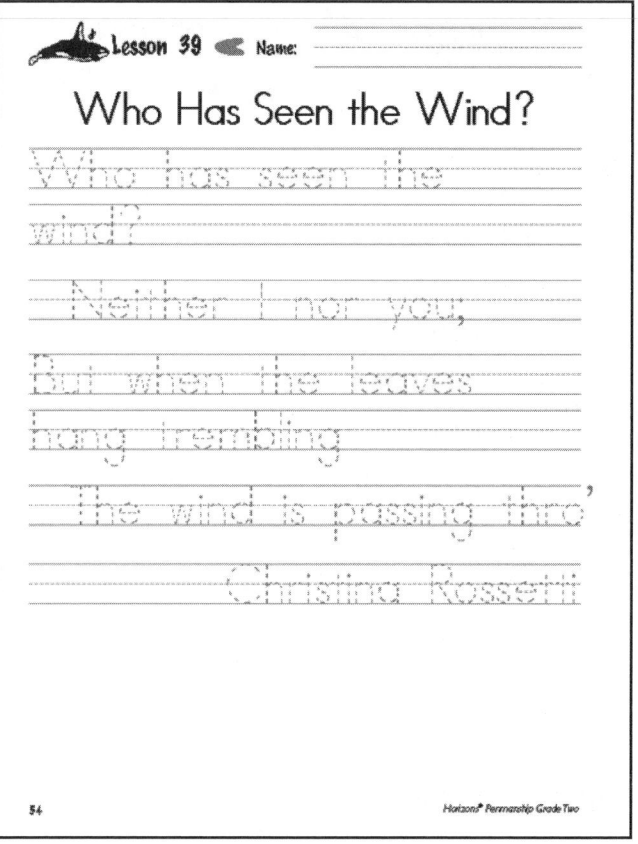

Lesson 40 - Special Page

Teaching Tips:

1. Explain that the children will copy the poem from Lesson 39 onto this special page using their best handwriting skills.
2. Allow the children to practice on the corresponding reproducible practice page from the back of this manual.
3. Complete the page.
4. Decide how this special page will be used.

Lesson 41 - Letters
O, o, F, f

Teaching Tips:

1. Talk about the name and the sounds each letter makes. Note how each letter is formed.

2. Warm up for each letter and word, check position.

3. Trace and copy the letters while the teacher observes the position, formation and spacing.

4. Additional blank lines may be used for practice, for original sentences, for class sentences, for phrases, for rhyming words and so on.

5. Quote for the week: from *The Wind* by Robert Louis Stevenson

The Wind

I saw you toss the kites on high
And blow the birds about the sky;
And all around I heard you pass,
Like ladies' skirts across the grass—
    O wind, a-blowing all day long,
    O wind, that sings so loud a song!

I saw the different things you did,
But always you yourself you hid.
I felt you push, I heard you call,
I could not see yourself at all—
    O wind, a-blowing all day long,
    O wind, that sings so loud a song!

O o   O o

F f   F f

cold

old

O you that are so strong and cold,
O blower, are you young or old?
Are you a beast of field and tree,
Or just a stronger child than me?
    O wind, a-blowing all day long,
    O wind, that sings so loud a
    song!

6. During the week read and discuss the entire poem drawing on the children's experiences with the wind.

7. Introduce new words: "a-blowing," "blower."

8. Blank lines in Lesson 41 may be used for additional words that rhyme with the sets on the page.

Lesson 42 - Practice Words

Teaching Tips:

1. Help the children with these words. Have them trace the word then practice writing it.
2. Watch formation and spacing.
3. During the week read and discuss the entire poem.
4. Blank lines in Lesson 42 may be used for additional words that rhyme with the sets on the page.

Poem for Lessons 41-45

"O you that are so strong and cold, O blower, are you young or old? Are you a beast of field and tree, Or just a stronger child than me? O wind, a-blowing all day long, O wind, that sings so loud a song!"

Lesson 43 - Practice Words

Teaching Tips:

1. Help the children with these words. Have them trace the word then practice writing it.
2. Watch formation and spacing.
3. During the week read and discuss the entire poem.
4. Work with new words: "a-blowing," "blower."
5. Additional blank lines may be used for practice, for original sentences, for class sentences, for phrases, for rhyming words and so on.

Lesson 42 Name:

tree

me

long

song

Lesson 43 Name:

beast

blower

a-blowing

stronger

Lesson 44 - Practice Poem

Teaching Tips:

1. Review the quote from Robert Louis Stevenson's poem **The Wind** with the children.

2. Discuss the meaning of this poem and the section that the children are to practice

3. Trace the quote.

4. Practice writing the quote for the week on a separate sheet of paper.

5. Give additional time for practicing this poem.

Poem for Lessons 41-45

"O you that are so strong and cold, O blower, are you young or old? Are you a beast of field and tree, Or just a stronger child than me? O wind, a-blowing all day long, O wind, that sings so loud a song!"

Lesson 45 - Special Page

Teaching Tips:

1. Explain that the children will copy the poem from Lesson 44 onto this special page using their best handwriting skills.

2. Allow the children to practice on the corresponding reproducible practice page from the back of this manual.

3. Give additional time to complete the final copying of this poem.

4. Complete the page.

5. Decide how this special page will be used.

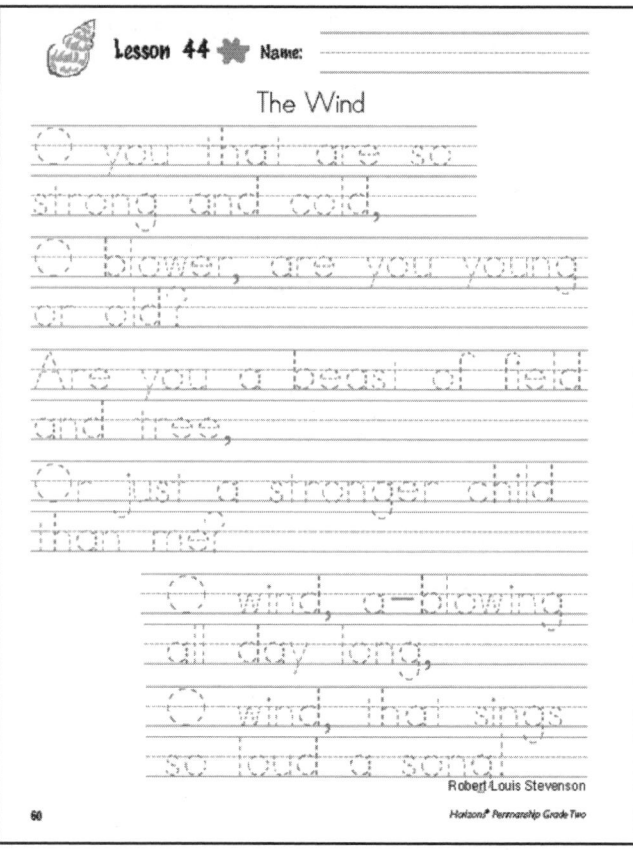

Lesson 46 - Letters
Q q, U, u

Teaching Tips:

1. Introduce the quote for the week: **I Kings 19:11.**

2. Read I Kings 19:11-13 to the children and discuss where Elijah found God (in the silent, gentle whisper).

3. Warm up for each letter and word, check position.

4. Trace and copy the letters and words while the teacher observes the position, formation and spacing.

5. Introduce any new or unfamiliar words: "shattered."

6. Additional blank lines may be used for practice, for original sentences, for class sentences, for phrases, for rhyming words, for last name practice and so on.

Bible Verse Lessons 46-50

"Then a great and powerful wind tore the mountains apart and shattered the rocks before the Lord, but the Lord was not in the wind." (I Kings 19:11)

Lesson 47 - Practice Words

Teaching Tips:

1. Help the children with these words. Have them trace the word then practice writing it.
2. Watch formation and spacing.
3. Additional blank lines may be used for practice, for original sentences, for class sentences, for phrases, for rhyming words and so on.

Bible Verse Lessons 46-50

"Then a great and powerful wind tore the mountains apart and shattered the rocks before the Lord, but the Lord was not in the wind." (I Kings 19:11)

Lesson 48 - Sentence Review

Teaching Tips:

1. Review sequence of letters and new words.
2. Help the children with these words. Have them trace the words then practice writing them.
3. Watch formation and spacing.

Lesson 47 ★ Name:

mountains

shattered rocks

tore apart

Kings

64   Horizons® Penmanship Grade Two

Lesson 48 ★ Name:

A great wind blew.

It tore mountains apart.

It shattered rocks.

The Lord was not

in the wind.

Horizons® Penmanship Grade Two   65

Lesson 49 - Practice Bible Verse

Teaching Tips:

1. Review **I Kings 19:11** with the children.
2. Discuss the meaning of this verse that the children are to practice
3. Trace the verse.
4. Practice writing the verse for the week on a separate sheet of paper.

Bible Verse Lessons 46-50

"Then a great and powerful wind tore the mountains apart and shattered the rocks before the Lord, but the Lord was not in the wind." (I Kings 19:11)

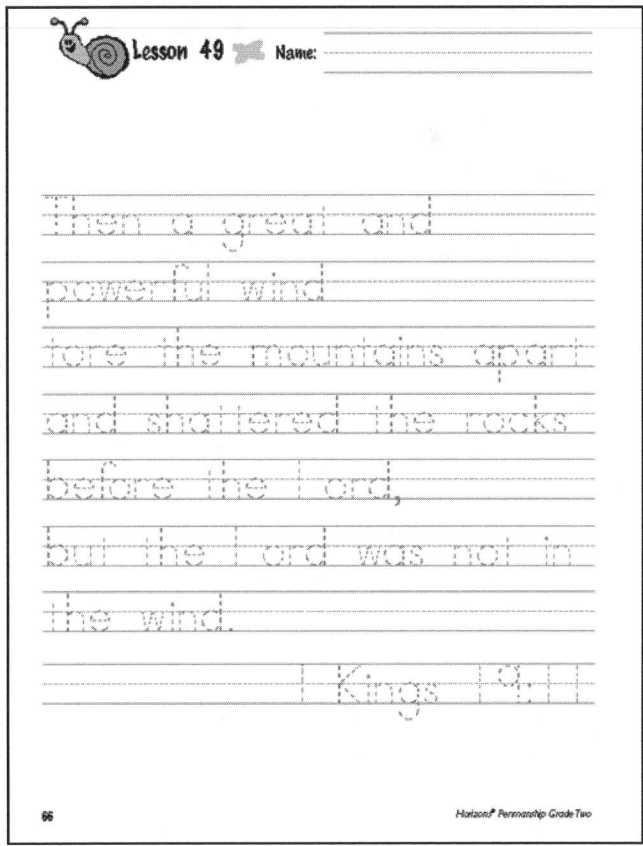

Lesson 50 - Special Page

Teaching Tips:

1. Explain that the children will copy the verse from Lesson 49 onto this special page using their best handwriting skills.
2. Allow the children to practice on the corresponding reproducible practice page from the back of this manual.
3. Complete the page.
4. Decide how this special page will be used.

Lesson 51 - Letters V, v X, x, Y, y, Z, z

Teaching Tips:

1. Talk about the name and the sounds each letter makes. Note how each letter is formed.

2. Warm up for each letter and check position.

3. Trace and copy the letters while the teacher observes the position, formation and spacing.

4. Additional blank lines may be used for practice.

5. Quote for the week: from *Spring Morning* by A. A. Milne

"Spring Morning"

Where am I going? I don't quite know.
Down to the stream where the king-cups
    grow—
Up on the hill where the pine-trees
    blow—
Anywhere, anywhere. I don't know.

Where am I going? The clouds sail by,
Little ones, baby ones, over the sky.
Where am I going? The shadows pass,
Little ones, baby ones, over the grass.

If you were a cloud and sailed up there,
You'd sail on water as blue as air,
And you'd see me here in the fields and
    say:
"Doesn't the sky look green today?"

Where am I going? The high rooks call:
"It's awful fun to be born at all."

Where am I going? The ring-doves coo:
"We do have beautiful things to do."
If you were a bird and lived on high,
You'd lean on the wind when the wind
    came by,
You'd say to the wind when it took you
    away:
"That's where I wanted to go today!"

Where am I going? I don't quite know.
What does it matter where people go?
Down to the wood where the blue-bells
    grow—
Anywhere, anywhere, I don't know.

6. During the week read the remaining verses of the poem and discuss with the children.

7. Introduce any words that may be new or unfamiliar.

Lesson 52 - Practice Words

Teaching Tips:

1. Help the children with these words. Have them trace the word then practice writing it.
2. Watch formation and spacing.
3. During the week read and discuss the entire poem.
4. Additional blank lines may be used for practice, for original sentences, for class sentences, for phrases, for rhyming words, for last name practice and so on.

Poem for Lessons 51-55

Spring Morning

"Where am I going? The clouds sail by, little ones, baby ones, over the sky. Where am I going? The shadows pass, Little ones, baby ones, over the grass."

Lesson 53 - Practice Words

Teaching Tips:

1. Help the children with these words. Have them trace the word then practice writing it.
2. Watch formation and spacing.
3. During the week read and discuss the entire poem.
4. Work with any new words.
5. Introduce the author's name.
6. Additional blank lines may be used for practice, for original sentences, for class sentences, for phrases, for rhyming words, for last name practice and so on.

Lesson 52   Name: _____

little ones

baby ones

shadows pass

over grass

70   Horizons® Penmanship Grade Two

Lesson 53   Name: _____

clouds sail by

over the sky

Where am I?

A. A. Milne

Horizons® Penmanship Grade Two   71

Lesson 54 - Practice Poem

Teaching Tips:

1. Review the quote from Robert Louis Stevenson's poem **Spring Morning** with the children.

2. Discuss the meaning of this poem and the section that the children are to practice.

3. Trace the quote.

4. Practice writing the quote for the week on a separate sheet of paper.

Poem for Lessons 51-55

Spring Morning

"Where am I going? The clouds sail by, little ones, baby ones, over the sky. Where am I going? The shadows pass, Little ones, baby ones, over the grass."

Lesson 55 - Special Page

Teaching Tips:

1. Explain that the children will copy the poem from Lesson 54 onto this special page using their best handwriting skills.

2. Allow the children to practice on the corresponding reproducible practice page from the back of this manual.

3. Complete the page.

4. Decide how this special page will be used.

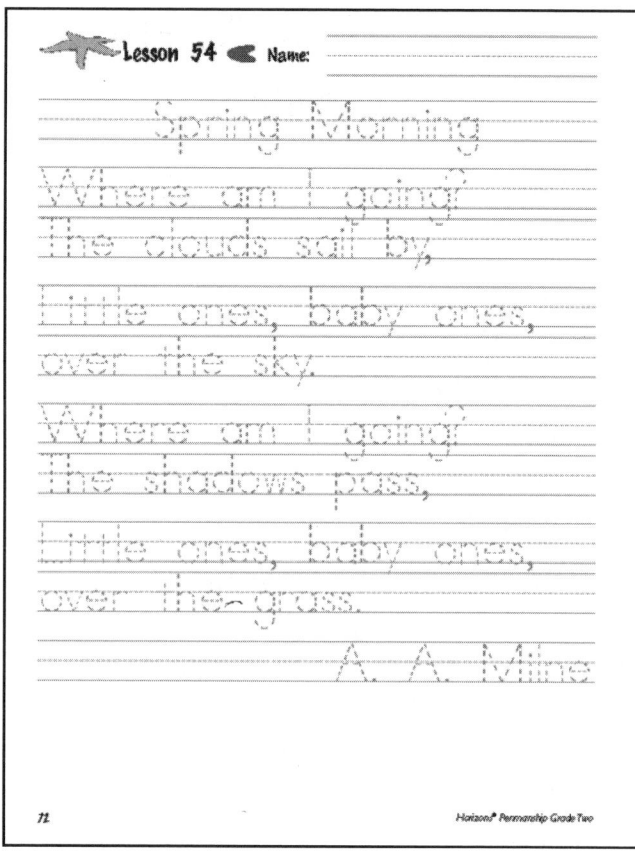

Lesson 56 - Practice Words

Teaching Tips:

1. Introduce the verse for the week: **Matthew 6:28-29.**

2. During the week read the contest for this verse: Matthew 6:25-34 and talk with the children about God's love and care for us and our need to always trust in the Lord for everything.

3. Warm up for each word and check position.

4. Trace and copy the words while the teacher observes the position, formation and spacing.

5. Introduce any words that maybe new or unfamiliar: "Solomon," Splendor."

6. Additional blank lines may be used for practice, for original sentences, for class sentences, for phrases, for rhyming words, for last name practice and so on.

Bible Verse Lessons 56-60

"See how the lilies of the field grow. They do not labor or spin. Yet I tell you that not even Solomon in all his splendor was dressed like one of these." (Matthew 6:28-29)

Lesson 56 ◄ Name:

see

spin

Solomon

splendor

Horizons Penmanship Grade Two 79

Lesson 57 - Practice Words & Phrases

Teaching Tips:

1. Help the children with these words. Have them trace the word then practice writing it.
2. Watch formation and spacing.
3. During the week read and discuss the verse.
4. Additional blank lines may be used for practice, for original sentences, for class sentences, for phrases, for rhyming words, for last name practice and so on.

Bible Verse Lessons 56-60

"See how the lilies of the field grow. They do not labor or spin. Yet I tell you that not even Solomon in all his splendor was dressed like one of these." (Matthew 6:28-29)

Lesson 58 - Practice Words & Sentences

Teaching Tips:

1. Help the children with these words. Have them trace the word then practice writing it.
2. Watch formation and spacing.
3. During the week read and discuss the verse.
4. Work with any new words.
5. Additional blank lines may be used for practice, for original sentences, for class sentences, for phrases, for rhyming words, for last name practice and so on.

lily

lilies

dressed like one

labor

field

they

these

They do not labor

or spin

Lesson 59 - Practice Bible Verse

Teaching Tips:

1. Review **Matthew 6:28:29** with the children.
2. Discuss the meaning of this verse that the children are to practice.
3. Trace the verse.
4. Practice writing the verse for the week on a separate sheet of paper.

Bible Verse Lessons 56-60

"See how the lilies of the field grow. They do not labor or spin. Yet I tell you that not even Solomon in all his splendor was dressed like one of these." (Matthew 6:28-29)

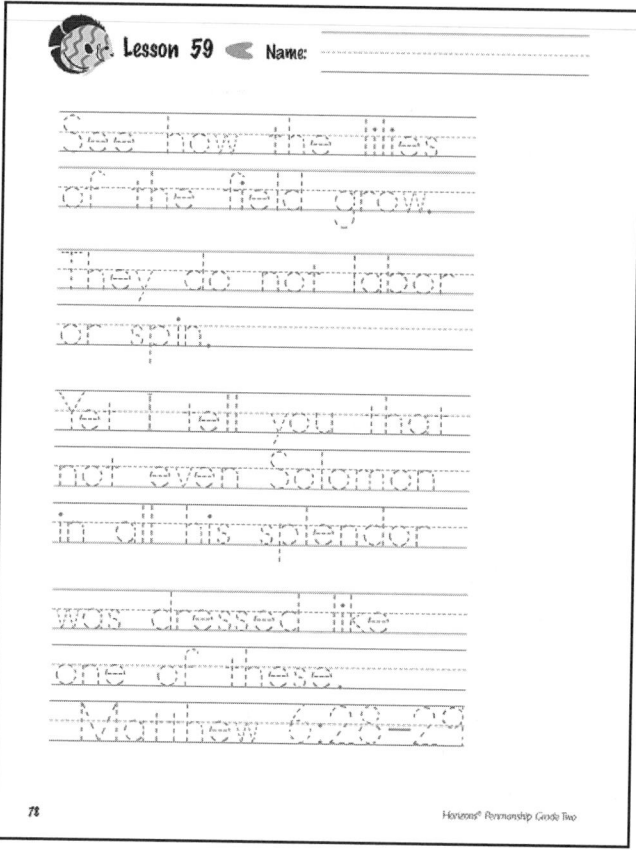

Lesson 60 - Special Page

Teaching Tips:

1. Explain that the children will copy the verse from Lesson 59 onto this special page using their best handwriting skills.
2. Allow the children to practice on the corresponding reproducible practice page from the back of this manual.
3. Complete the page.
4. Decide how this special page will be used.

Lesson 61 - Practice Words

Teaching Tips:

1. Help the children with these words. Have them trace the word then practice writing it.
2. Watch formation and spacing.
3. Quote for the week: from *I Wandered Lonely as a Cloud* by William Wordsworth

I Wandered Lonely as a Cloud

I WANDERED lonely as a cloud
That floats on high o'er vales and hills,
When all at once I saw a crowd,
A host, of golden daffodils;

Beside the lake, beneath the trees,
Fluttering and dancing in the breeze.
Continuous as the stars that shine
And twinkle on the milky way,

They stretched in never-ending line
Along the margin of a bay: 10
Ten thousand saw I at a glance,
Tossing their heads in sprightly dance.

The waves beside them danced; but they
Out-did the sparkling waves in glee:
A poet could not but be gay,
In such a jocund company:

I gazed—and gazed—but little thought
What wealth the show to me had brought:
For oft, when on my couch I lie
In vacant or in pensive mood,   20
They flash upon that inward eye
Which is the bliss of solitude;
And then my heart with pleasure fills,
And dances with the daffodils.

Lesson 61 ★ Name:

over

o'er

vale

valley

Horizons® Penmanship Grade Two   81

4. Begin writing the quote out in cursive as well as manuscript and having the children compare the cursive and manuscript forms.
5. Throughout the week read additional stanzas from the poem. Ask the children what they might see if they wandered overhead like a cloud.
6. Introduce new or unfamiliar words: "o'er," "vales," "host," "daffodils."
7. Additional blank lines may be used for practice, for original sentences, for class sentences, for phrases, for rhyming words, for last name practice and so on.

Lesson 62 - Practice Words

Teaching Tips:

1. Help the children with these words. Have them trace the word then practice writing it.
2. Watch formation and spacing.
3. Read additional stanzas from the poem.
4. Additional blank lines may be used for practice, for original sentences, for class sentences, for phrases, for rhyming words, for last name practice and so on.

Poem for Lessons 61-65

"I WANDERED lonely as a cloud That floats on high o'er vales and hills, When all at once I saw a crowd, A host, of golden daffodils;"

wandered

crowd

hills

daffodils

82   Horizons® Penmanship Grade Two

Lesson 63 - Sentence Review

Teaching Tips:

1. Review sequences of letters and new words.
2. Help the children with these words. Have them trace the words then practice writing them.
3. Watch formation and spacing.
4. Talk about the meaning of the sentences.
5. Additional blank lines may be used for practice, for original sentences, for class sentences, for phrases, for rhyming words, for last name practice and so on.

A cloud floats high.

A host is a crowd.

Daffodils are golden yellow.

A vale is a valley.

Horizons® Penmanship Grade Two   83

Lesson 64 - Practice Poem

Teaching Tips:

1. Review the quote from Robert Louis Stevenson's poem **I Wandered Lonely as a Cloud** with the children.
2. Discuss the meaning of this poem and the section that the children are to practice.
3. Trace the quote.
4. Practice writing the quote for the week on a separate sheet of paper.

Poem for Lessons 61-65

"I WANDERED lonely as a cloud That floats on high o'er vales and hills, When all at once I saw a crowd, A host, of golden daffodils;"

Lesson 65 - Special Page

Teaching Tips:

1. Explain that the children will copy the poem from Lesson 64 onto this special page using their best handwriting skills.
2. Allow the children to practice on the corresponding reproducible practice page from the back of this manual.
3. Complete the page.
4. Decide how this special page will be used.

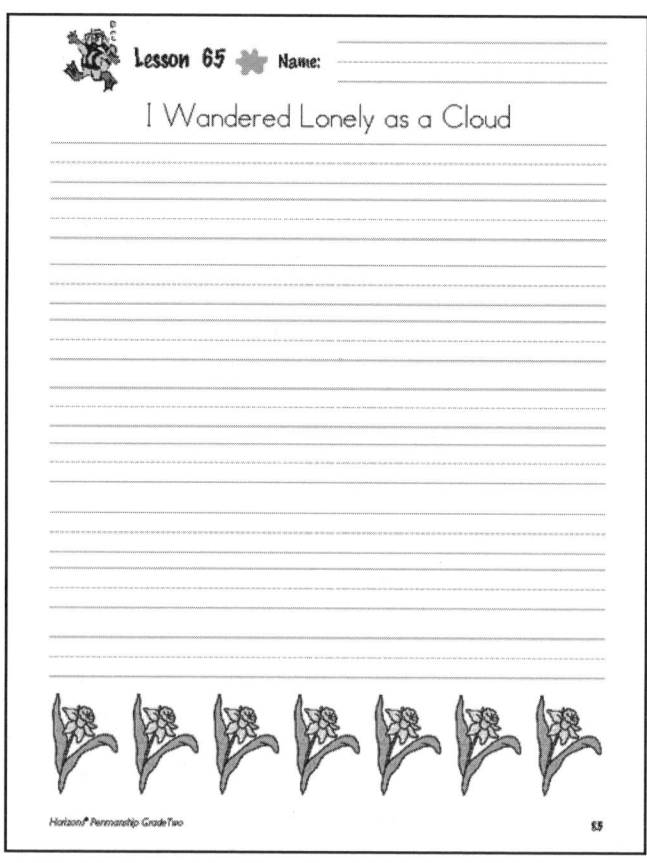

Lesson 66 - Practice Words

Teaching Tips:

1. Help the children with these words. Have them trace the word then practice writing it.

2. Watch formation and spacing.

3. Quote for the week: from *Oh, Fair to See* by Christina Rossetti

Oh, Fair to See

Oh, fair to see
Bloom-laden cherry tree,
    Arrayed in sunny white:
    An April day's delight,
Oh, fair to see!

Oh, fair to see
Fruit-laden cherry tree,
    With balls of shining red
    Decking a leafy head,
Oh, fair to see!

4. During the week read the other stanza. Talk about the tree in bloom and the tree with fruit on it. Find pictures if you are able.

5. Introduce new or unfamiliar words or phrases: "leafy head," "fruit-laden," "decking."

6. Additional blank lines may be used for practice, for original sentences, for class sentences, for phrases, for rhyming words, for last name practice and so on.

Lesson 66   Name:

see tree

red head

fruit-laden

cherry tree

Horizons® Penmanship Grade Two   87

Lesson 67 - Practice Phrases & Sentences

Teaching Tips:

1. Help the children with these words. Have them trace the word then practice writing it.
2. Watch formation and spacing.
3. During the week read and discuss the verse.
4. Additional blank lines may be used for practice, for original sentences, for class sentences, for phrases, for rhyming words and so on.

Poem for Lessons 66-70

Oh, Fair to See

"Oh, fair to see Fruit-laden cherry tree, With balls of shining red Decking a leafy head, Oh, fair to see!"

Lesson 68 - Practice Words & Phrases

Teaching Tips:

1. Help the children with these words. Have them trace the word then practice writing it.
2. Watch formation and spacing.
3. During the week read and discuss the verse.
4. Discuss writing titles and the use of capital letters for the main words in the title.
5. Additional blank lines may be used for practice, for original sentences, for class sentences, for phrases, for rhyming words and so on.

Lesson 67   Name:

balls of shining red

decking a leafy head

Cherries are red.

They are fair to see.

Horizons® Penmanship Grade Two

Lesson 68   Name:

Christina

Rossetti

Oh, Fair to See

Horizons® Penmanship Grade Two

Lesson 69 - Practice Poem

Teaching Tips:

1. Review the quote from Robert Louis Stevenson's poem **Oh, Fair to See** with the children.

2. Discuss the meaning of this poem and the section that the children are to practice.

3. Trace the quote.

4. Practice writing the quote for the week on a separate sheet of paper.

Poem for Lessons 66-70

Oh, Fair to See

"Oh, fair to see Fruit-laden cherry tree, With balls of shining red Decking a leafy head, Oh, fair to see!"

Lesson 70 - Special Page

Teaching Tips:

1. Explain that the children will copy the poem from Lesson 69 onto this special page using their best handwriting skills.

2. Allow the children to practice on the corresponding reproducible practice page from the back of this manual.

3. Complete the page.

4. Decide how this special page will be used.

Lesson 71 - Practice Words

Teaching Tips:

1. Introduce the verse for the week: **Song of Songs 2:11-12**.

2. Find and read other appropriate nature references from Song of Songs during the week.

3. Warm up for each word and check position.

4. Trace and copy the words while the teacher observes the position, formation and spacing.

5. Introduce new or unfamiliar words: "cooing," "coo," "season."

6. Additional blank lines may be used for practice, for original sentences, for class sentences, for phrases, for rhyming words, for last name practice and so on.

Bible Verse Lessons 71-75

"See! The winter is past; the rains are over and gone. Flowers appear on the earth; the season of singing has come, the cooing of doves is heard in our land."
(Song of Songs 2:11-12)

Lesson 71   Name:

season

singing

cooing

Song of Songs

Horizons® Penmanship Grade Two   94

Lesson 72 - Sentence Review

Teaching Tips:

1. Review sequences of letters and new words.
2. Help the children with these words. Have them trace the words then practice writing them.
3. Watch formation and spacing.
4. Additional blank lines may be used for practice, for original sentences, for class sentences, for phrases, for rhyming words and so on.

Bible Verse Lessons 71-75

"See! The winter is past; the rains are over and gone. Flowers appear on the earth; the season of singing has come, the cooing of doves is heard in our land."
(Song of Songs 2:11-12)

Lesson 73 - Sentence Review

Teaching Tips:

1. Review sequences of letters and new words.
2. Help the children with these words. Have them trace the words then practice writing them.
3. Watch formation and spacing.
4. Stress that proper nouns like "God" and the names of people begin with capital letters.

Lesson 72 ◄ Name:

The winter is past.

The rains are over.

The rains are gone.

Flowers appear.

94   Horizons® Penmanship Grade Two

Lesson 73 ◄ Name:

The season has come to

sing. Doves coo

in the land. We hear

the doves cooing.

We praise God.

Horizons® Penmanship Grade Two   95

Lesson 74 - Practice Bible Verse

Teaching Tips:

1. Review **Song of Songs 2:11-12** with the children.
2. Discuss the meaning of this verse that the children are to practice.
3. Trace the verse.
4. Practice writing the verse for the week on a separate sheet of paper.

Bible Verse Lessons 71-75

"See! The winter is past; the rains are over and gone. Flowers appear on the earth; the season of singing has come, the cooing of doves is heard in our land."
(Song of Songs 2:11-12)

Lesson 75 - Special Page

Teaching Tips:

1. Explain that the children will copy the verse from Lesson 49 onto this special page using their best handwriting skills.
2. Allow the children to practice on the corresponding reproducible practice page from the back of this manual.
3. Complete the page.
4. Decide how this special page will be used.

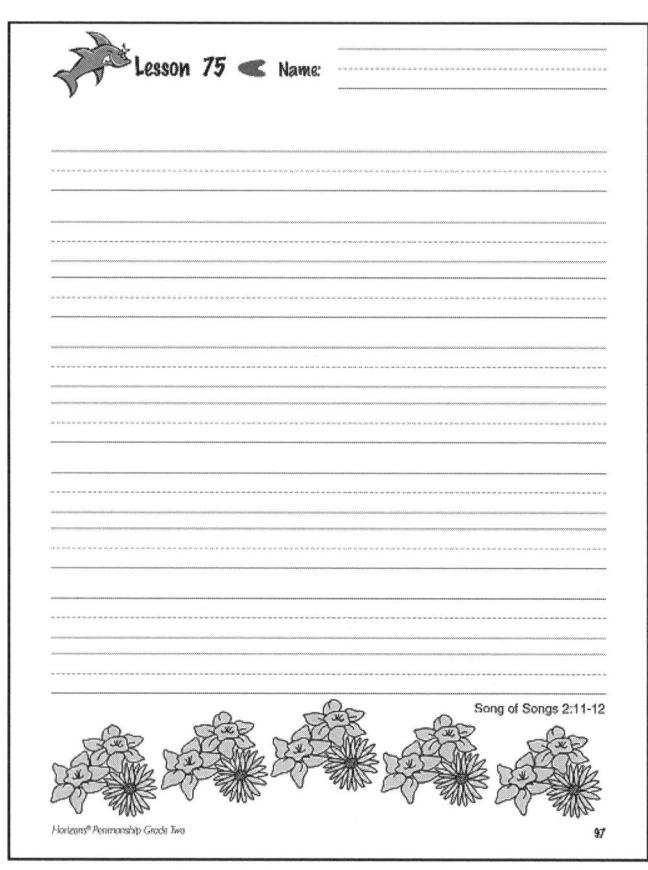

Lessons 76-80 Introduction to Cursive Writing: Aa, Cc, Oo.

If cursive readiness has been fostered throughout the first half of this year (see general introduction), the children should be visually ready to begin cursive writing. Some children may still lack the skills for good manuscript writing and may not be ready to move on to cursive writing. For those students who are not ready, alternate lessons are provided at the end of this Teacher's Guide.

Lesson 76 - Introduction to Cursive Letters

1. Quote for the week: **Psalm 23:1-2**. Read it with the children. Have a copy posted for them to see each day. Prepare a parallel cursive copy and ask the children to begin making comparisons between the two as they learn new letters.

2. Introduce cursive letter formation in the same manner used to introduce the manuscript alphabet:

   Say the letter.

   Form it in the air.

   Describe the formation as it is written noting its slant, position and size within the guidelines. Descriptions are given in the lessons and are meant to accompany the demonstration of the letter, not to be used in isolation.

   Have the children practice writing the letter in the air, on their hands, on the board, etc.

Use tactile materials such as sand or salt, finger paints or clay to allow the children to trace or form the letters.

3. Introduce the first cursive letter: **Aa**.

4. Note that both the capital and small letters are formed in the same manner. The only difference is the size: The capital "A" is two spaces tall and begins on the top line; the small "a" is only one space tall and begins at the dotted line. Note that the final up stroke on both letters end at the dotted line.

5. Note the slant of the letter and the oval rather than round shape.

Bible Verse Lessons 76-80

"The Lord is my Shepherd, I shall not want. He makes me lie down in green pastures, he leads me beside quiet waters, he restores my soul." (Psalm 23:1-2)

Alternate Lesson 76 - Practice Words & Sentences

Teaching Tips:

1. Help the children with these words. Have them trace the word then practice writing it.

2. Watch formation and spacing.

3. During the week read and discuss the verse. Students doing the alternate lessons will be writing the same verse or poem that the students doing cursive write.

4. Additional blank lines may be used for practice, for original sentences, for class sentences, for phrases, for rhyming words and so on.

5. If an Alternate Lesson is not provided then all students should do the regular lesson.

Alternate Lesson 76

shepherd

pastures

quiet

The Lord is my shepherd

Horizons Penmanship Grade Two

Lesson 77 - Introduction to Cursive Letter C, c

Teaching Tips:

1. Read additional verses from **Psalm 23**.

2. Introduce the cursive letter: **Cc**.

3. Note that both capital and small are formed in the same manner. The difference is the size: the capital "C" is two spaces tall and begins just below the top line. It moves up, around, down and back up to the dotted line. The small "c" begins just below the dotted line and moves up, around, down and back up and out to the dotted line.

4. Compare the shape and slant to the manuscript letter.

Bible Verse Lessons 76-80

"The Lord is my Shepherd, I shall not want. He makes me lie down in green pastures, he leads me beside quiet waters, he restores my soul." (Psalm 23:1-2)

Alternate Lesson 77 - Practice Sentences

Teaching Tips:

1. Help the children with these sentences. Have them trace the word then practice writing it.

2. Watch formation and spacing.

3. During the week read and discuss the verse.

4. Additional blank lines may be used for practice, for original sentences, for class sentences, for phrases, for rhyming words and so on.

Lesson 78 - Introduction to Cursive Letter O, o

Teaching Tips:

1. Read all of **Psalm 23** as a prayer.

2. Introduce the cursive letter: **Oo**.

3. The formation of the capital and small letter has two differences: the size and the final loop at the top of the capital "O." The capital letter goes all the way around, then loops back down, up and out. The small letter moves back out and up at the end, but without a loop.

4. Compare slant and shape with the manuscript letter. (Make this comparison with each letter introduced.)

Bible Verse Lessons 76-80

"The Lord is my Shepherd, I shall not want. He makes me lie down in green pastures, he leads me beside quiet waters, he restores my soul." (Psalm 23:1-2)

Alternate Lesson 78 - Practice Sentences

Teaching Tips:

1. Help the children with these sentences. Have them trace the word then practice writing it.

2. Watch formation and spacing.

3. During the week read and discuss the verse.

4. Additional blank lines may be used for practice, for original sentences, for class sentences, for phrases, for rhyming words and so on.

Lesson 79 - Practice Bible Verse

Teaching Tips:

1. Introduce new or unfamiliar words.
2. Practice **Psalm 23:1-2.**
3. Watch formation and spacing

Bible Verse Lessons 76-80

"The Lord is my Shepherd, I shall not want. He makes me lie down in green pastures, he leads me beside quiet waters, he restores my soul." (Psalm 23:1-2)

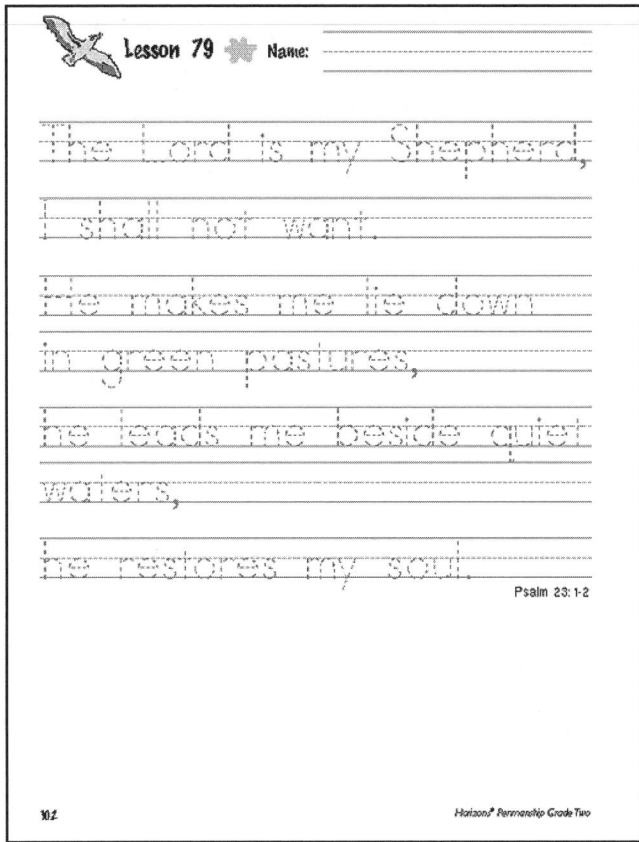

Lesson 80 - Special Page

Teaching Tips:

1. Explain that the children will copy the verse from Lesson 79 onto this special page using their best handwriting skills.
2. Allow the children to practice on the corresponding reproducible practice page from the back of this manual.
3. Complete final copy.
4. Decide how this special page will be used.

Lessons 81-85 Introduction to Cursive Writing: Dd, Qq, Gg.

If cursive readiness has been fostered throughout the first half of this year (see general introduction), the children should be visually ready to begin cursive writing. If some children lack the skills for good manuscript writing, they may not be ready to move on to cursive writing. For those students who are not ready, alternate lessons are provided at the end of this Teacher's Guide.

Lesson 81 - Introduction to Cursive Letter Dd

Teaching Tips:

1. Quote for the week: from **Spring Morning** by A. A. Milne Students should remember this poem from Lessons 51 – 55.

"Spring Morning"

Where am I going? I don't quite know.
Down to the stream where the king-cups grow—
Up on the hill where the pine-trees blow—
Anywhere, anywhere. I don't know.

Where am I going? The clouds sail by,
Little ones, baby ones, over the sky.
Where am I going? The shadows pass,
Little ones, baby ones, over the grass.

If you were a cloud and sailed up there,
You'd sail on water as blue as air,
And you'd see me here in the fields and say:
"Doesn't the sky look green today?"

Where am I going" The high rooks call:
It's awful fun to be born at all."
Where am I going? The ring-doves coo:
"We do have beautiful things to do."

If you were a bird and lived on high,
You'd lean on the wind when the wind came by,
You'd say to the wind when it took you away:
"That's where I wanted to go today!"

Where am I going? I don't quite know.
What does it matter where people go?
Down to the wood where the blue-bells grow—
Anywhere, anywhere, I don't know.

2. Reread the poem with the children.

3. Introduce the cursive letter: **Dd**.

4. The capital and small letter are both two spaces tall. The capital "D" begins at the top line, goes down on a slant to the bottom line, loops up, around and back down to the line, then curves up to the top and loops around and out.

5. The small "d" begins at the dotted line (just like the small "a"), moves around and up to the top line, back down again to the bottom line and curves up to end at the dotted line.

Alternate Lesson 81 - Practice Words & ?

Teaching Tips:

1. Help the children with these words and the question mark. Have them trace these then practice writing them.

2. Watch formation and spacing.

3. During the week read and discuss the verse.

4. Additional blank lines may be used for practice, for original sentences, for class sentences, for phrases, for rhyming words and so on.

Alternate Lesson 81

anywhere

blue=bells

? ? ? ?

Lesson 82 - Introduction to Cursive Letter Q q

Teaching Tips:

1. Introduce the cursive letter: **Qq**.
2. The capital and small letters are very different. Both are two spaces, but the small letter goes down into the space below the line.
3. The capital "Q" is made from the bottom up (unlike the manuscript "Q"). Begin at the bottom line, go around (clockwise) to the top line and back down again. Make a loop around and out along the bottom line to complete.
4. The small "q" begins like the small "a" and "d" but it drops a space below the line, then loops around the back and up touching the bottom line, then continuing up to the dotted line.

Poem for Lessons 81-85

"Where am I going? I don't quite know. What does it matter where people go? Down to the wood where the blue-bells grow— Anywhere, anywhere, I don't know."

Alternate Lesson 82 - Practice Sentences

Teaching Tips:

1. Help the children with these sentences. Have them trace these then practice writing them.
2. Watch formation and spacing.
3. Read and discuss the poem.
4. Additional blank lines may be used for practice, sentences, words and so on.

Lesson 82 Name:

Q Q Q Q

q q q q

Q

q

cod cod

Alternate Lesson 82

Where am I going?

Where are you going?

What does it matter?

Lesson 83: Introduction to Cursive Letter G, g

Teaching Tips:

1. Introduce the cursive letter: **Gg**.

2. Note the slant on the capital "G." Begin at the bottom and slant up and forward all the way to the top line. Loop back around, down to the dotted line, curve back up to the top line again. Then drop down to the bottom, around and back up across the first line to the dotted line and back in to the center. The final stroke resembles a "smile."

3. The small "g" begins like the small "a" "d" and "q." It drops a space below the line, then loops around the front and back up across the line all the way to the dotted line without stopping like the small "q" had to do.

Poem for Lessons 81-85

"Where am I going? I don't quite know. What does it matter where people go? Down to the wood where the blue-bells grow— Anywhere, anywhere, I don't know."

Alternate Lesson 83 - Practice Sentences

Teaching Tips:

1. Help the children with these sentences. Have them trace these then practice writing them.

2. Watch formation and spacing.

3. Read and discuss the poem.

4. Additional blank lines may be used for practice sentences, words and so on.

Lesson 84 - Poem

Teaching Tips:

1. Introduce any new or unfamiliar words: "blue-bells." Note the contraction "don't," and the compound-word "anywhere."
2. Practice the quote.
3. Watch spacing and letter formation.

Poem for Lessons 81-85

"Where am I going? I don't quite know. What does it matter where people go? Down to the wood where the blue-bells grow— Anywhere, anywhere, *I* don't know."

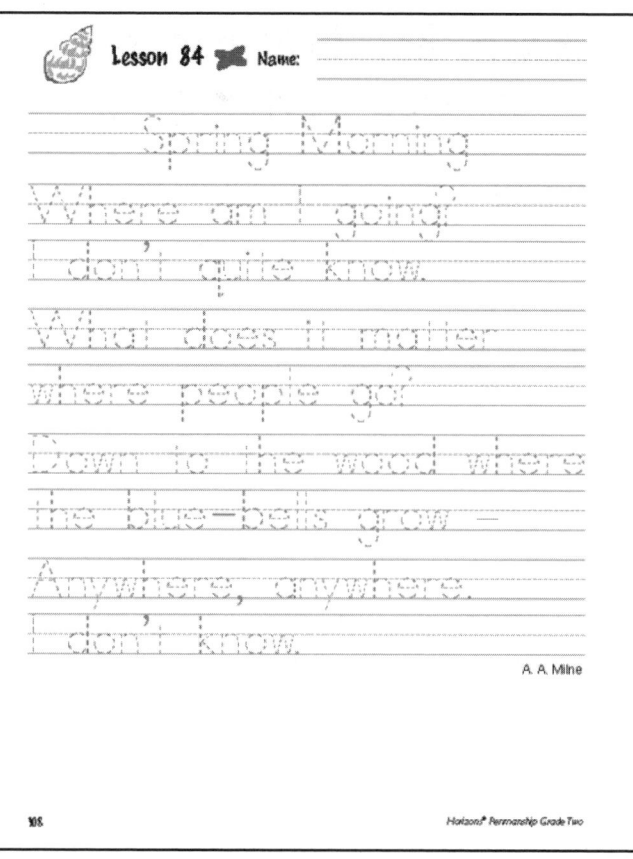

Lesson 85 - Special Page

Teaching Tips:

1. Explain that the children will copy the poem from Lesson 84 onto this special page using their best handwriting skills.
2. Allow the children to practice on the corresponding reproducible practice page from the back of this manual.
3. Complete the final copy of the quote.
4. Decide how this special page will be used.

Lesson 86: Introduction to Cursive Letter E, e

Teaching Tips:

1. Quote for the week: **Psalm 148:7-8**.

2. Introduce the cursive letter: **Ee**.

3. The capital "E" begins just a pencil point below the top line, curves up and around to the dotted line where it makes a small loop before continuing around and down to the bottom line and back up to the ending point at the dotted line.

4. The small "e" begins on the bottom line, curves up to the dotted line where it loops around and down to the bottom line, then up to the ending point at the dotted line.

5. Continue to note the differences and similarities between the manuscript and cursive letters.

Bible Verse Lessons 86-90

"Praise the Lord from the earth, you sea creatures and all ocean depths, lightning and hail, snow and clouds, stormy winds that do his bidding," (Psalm 148:7-8)

Alternate Lesson 86 - Practice Phrases

Teaching Tips:

1. Help the children with these phrases. Have them trace these then practice writing them.

2. Watch formation and spacing.

3. Read and discuss the verse.

4. Additional blank lines may be used for practice phrases, words and so on.

Lesson 87 - Introduction to Cursive Letter B, b

Teaching Tips:

1. Read additional verses from **Psalm 148**.

2. Introduce the cursive letter: **Bb**

3. The capital "B" begins at the dotted line with an upstroke, moves up to the top line, then down to the bottom line and back up again. Just before it touches the top line it curves up and around, makes a small loop at the dotted line, then curves around the bottom line, up to touch the down stroke and back in with a little "smile."

4. The small "b" begins with an up stroke that moves from the bottom line all the way to the top line, loops up and back down to the bottom. When it reaches the bottom line it curves forward and immediately back up to the dotted line, then ends with a small curved stroke on the dotted line.

Alternate Lesson 87 - Practice Phrases

Teaching Tips:

1. Help the children with these phrases. Have them trace these then practice writing them.

2. Watch formation and spacing.

3. Read and discuss the verse.

4. Additional blank lines may be used for practice phrases, words and so on.

B B B B

b b b b

B

b

bed bed

Alternate Lesson 87

snow and clouds

stormy winds

do his bidding

Lesson 88 - Cursive Letter Review

Teaching Tips:

1. Read all of **Psalm 148**.
2. Review cursive letters. Note position, formation and slant of letters and words.

Bible Verse Lessons 86-90

"Praise the Lord from the earth, you sea creatures and all ocean depths, lightning and hail, snow and clouds, stormy winds that do his bidding," (Psalm 148:7-8)

Lesson 88 Name:

Aa Bb Cc Dd

Ee Gg Oo Qq

do do

God God

dog dog dog

Horizons® Penmanship Grade Two

Alternate Lesson 88 - Practice Sentences

Teaching Tips:

1. Help the children with these sentences. Have them trace these then practice writing them.
2. Watch formation and spacing.
3. Read and discuss the verse.
4. Additional blank lines may be used for practice sentences, words and so on.

Alternate Lesson 88

Praise the Lord from

the earth.

Things of the earth

that praise the Lord.

Horizons® Penmanship Grade Two

Lesson 89 - Bible Verse

Teaching Tips:

1. Introduce any new or unfamiliar words.
2. Practice the **Psalm 148:7-8**.

Bible Verse Lessons 86-90

"Praise the Lord from the earth, you sea creatures and ocean depths, lightning and hail, snow and clouds, stormy winds that do his bidding ..." (Psalm 148:7-8)

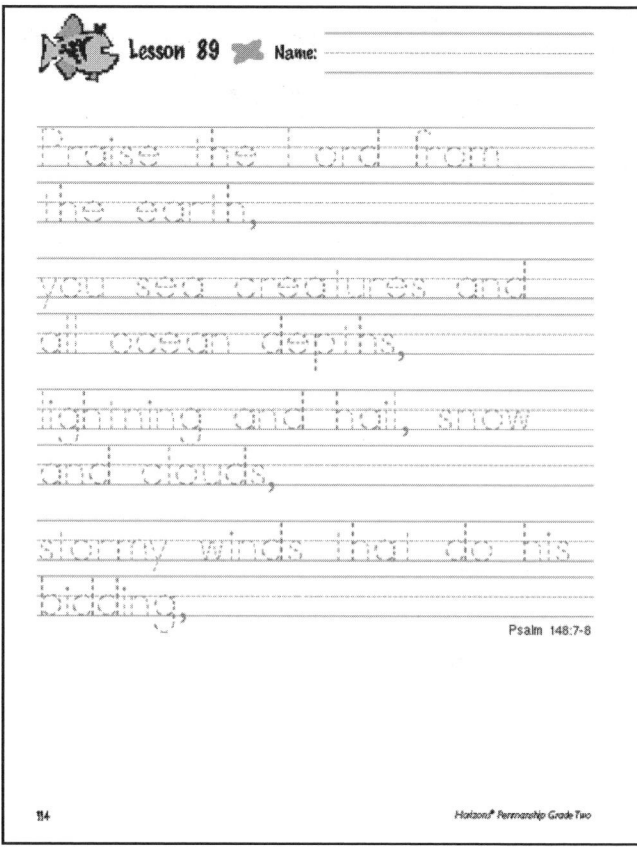

Lesson 90 - Special Page

Teaching Tips:

1. Explain that the children will copy the verse from Lesson 89 onto this special page using their best handwriting skills.
2. Allow the children to practice on the corresponding reproducible practice page from the back of this manual.
3. Complete the final copy of the verse.
4. Decide how this special page will be used.

Lesson 91 - Introduction to Cursive Letter H, h

Teaching Tips:

1. Quote for the week: **Psalm 148:7, 9-10.**

2. Introduce the cursive letter: **Hh.**

3. The capital "H" is the first cursive letter introduced to use two separate strokes. The first stroke begins at the top line, then moves gently around and down to the bottom line. The second stroke begins at the top line, then moves gently back, around and down to the bottom line where it curves back up to the dotted line and ends in a loop that touches the first stroke below the dotted line and continues to the dotted line.

4. The small "h" begins like the small "b" with an upstroke from the bottom to top and a loop around and back down to the bottom. When it touches the bottom line it moves up in an arch to the dotted line, then back down to the bottom. It touches the bottom line and moves into a final upstroke that ends at the dotted line.

Bible Verse Lessons 91-95

"Praise the Lord … you mountains and all the hills, fruit trees and all cedars, wild animals and all cattle, small creatures and flying birds … " (Psalm 148:7, 9-10)

Alternate Lesson 91 - Practice Words & Phrases

Teaching Tips:

1. Help the children with these word and phrases. Have them trace these then practice writing them.

2. Watch formation and spacing.

3. Read and discuss the verse.

4. Additional blank lines may be used for practice phrases, words and so on.

Alternate Lesson 91

fruit trees and cedars

wild animals

cattle

Lesson 92 - Introduction to Cursive Letter K, k

Teaching Tips:

1. Pray **Psalm 148: 1-6**.

2. Introduce the cursive letter: **Kk**.

3. The capital "K" is another two-stroke letter. The first stroke is identical to the first stroke of the capital "H." The second stroke begins at the top line, curves in to meet the first stroke at the dotted line, then moves down and slightly out to the bottom line and moves into a final upstroke that ends at the dotted line.

4. The small "k" begins like the small "h" and "b" with an upstroke from the bottom to top and a loop around and back down to the bottom. When it touches the bottom line it retraces its steps to the dotted line, then makes a loop (below the dotted line) and curves back down to the bottom line and up to the end point on the dotted line.

Bible Verse Lessons 91-95

"Praise the Lord ... you mountains and all the hills, fruit trees and all cedars, wild animals and all cattle, small creatures and flying birds ... " (Psalm 148:7, 9-10)

Alternate Lesson 92 - Practice Phrases

Teaching Tips:

1. Help the children with these phrases. Have them trace these then practice writing them.

2. Watch formation and spacing.

3. Read and discuss the verse.

4. Additional blank lines may be used for practice phrases, words and so on.

small creatures

flying birds

all the hills

Lesson 93 - Introduction to Cursive Letter I, i

Teaching Tips:

1. Read **Psalm 148:7-14**.

2. Introduce the cursive letter: **Ii**.

3. The formation of the capital "I" moves "backwards" when compared to the other letters. It begins on the bottom line, curves back around and up to touch the top line before curving back down again. When it reaches the bottom line it continues its curve back and up to the dotted line, then back in with a "smile."

4. The small "i" is a two-stroke letter. It begins like the small "e" with an upstroke from the bottom line to the dotted line. It then retraces its steps down to the bottom line and ends with an upstroke to the dotted line (like the small "e" without a loop). The second stroke is the dot placed above the letter in the middle of the top space.

Bible Verse Lessons 91-95

"Praise the Lord … you mountains and all the hills, fruit trees and all cedars, wild animals and all cattle, small creatures and flying birds … " (Psalm 148:7, 9-10)

Alternate Lesson 93 - Practice Sentences

Teaching Tips:

1. Help the children with these sentences. Have them trace these then practice writing them.

2. Watch formation and spacing.

3. Read and discuss the verse.

4. Additional blank lines may be used for practice sentences, phrases, words and so on.

I praise the Lord.

All creation praises the Lord.

How do you praise the Lord?

Lesson 94 - Bible Verse &

Teaching Tips:

1. Introduce new or unfamiliar words.
2. Practice **Psalm 148:7, 9-10**.

Bible Verse Lessons 91-95

"Praise the Lord … you mountains and all the
hills, fruit trees and all cedars, wild animals and
all cattle, small creatures and flying birds … "
(Psalm 148:7, 9-10)

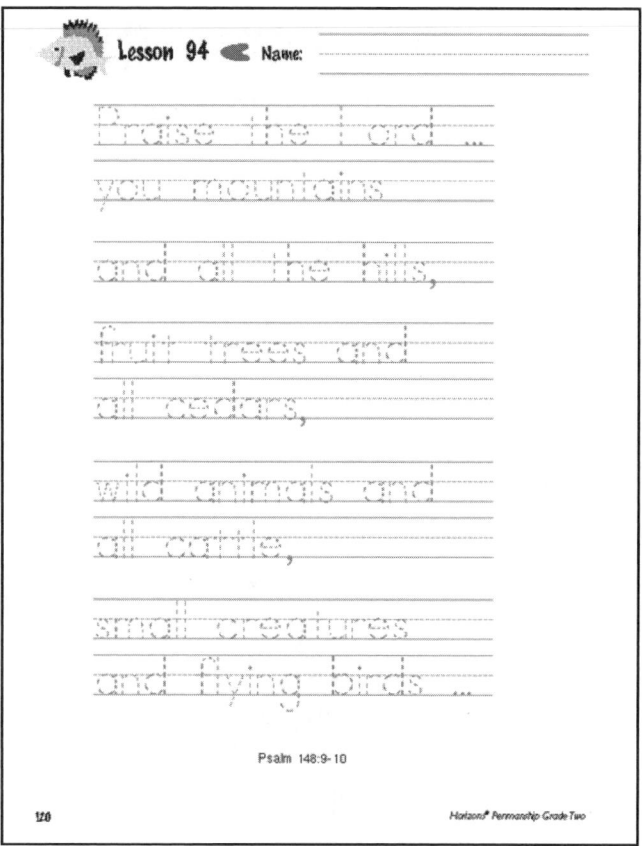

Lesson 95 - Special Page

Teaching Tips:

1. Explain that the children will copy the
   verse from Lesson 94 onto this special
   page using their best handwriting skills.
2. Allow the children to practice on the
   corresponding reproducible practice
   page from the back of this manual.
3. Complete final copy.
4. Decide how this special page will be
   used.

Lesson 96 - Introduction to Cursive Letter T, t

Teaching Tips:

1. Quote for the week: **When Fishes Set Umbrellas Up** by Christina Rossetti. (The entire poem is the quote for the week.)

2. Introduce the cursive letter: **Tt**.

3. The capital "T" is a two-stroke letter. The first stroke "waves" along the top line. It begins with a very tiny line down from the top line that curves immediately back up along the top line (touching the top line in three places). The second stroke begins in the middle of this "wavy" line and curves down to the bottom line, around, back, up to the dotted line and in with a "smile."

4. The small "t" is also a two-stroke letter. It begins with a tall upstroke from the bottom line to the top line, traces itself back down to the bottom line, around and up to the end point on the dotted line. The second stroke is a short cross bar that is placed just ABOVE the dotted line.

Poem for Lessons 96-100

When Fishes Set Umbrellas Up

"When fishes set umbrellas up
If rain-drops run,
Lizards will want their parasols
To shade them from the sun."

Alternate Lesson 96 - Practice Words

Teaching Tips:

1. Help the children with these words. Have them trace these then practice writing them.

2. Watch formation and spacing.

3. Read and discuss the poem.

4. Additional blank lines may be used for practice phrases, words and so on.

rain-drops

umbrellas

parasols

Lesson 97 - Introduction to Cursive Letter F, f

Teaching Tips:

1. Reread poem for the week.
2. Introduce the cursive letter: **Ff**.
3. The capital "F" is a three-stroke letter. The first and second strokes are identical to the capital "T" described in Lesson 96. The third stroke is a short cross stroke on the dotted line.
4. The small "f" is a "three-story" letter. It begins like the small "b," "h," and "k" with an upstroke from the bottom line to the top line that loops back around and down. The down line moves all the way down one space below the bottom line before looping back up to touch the bottom line and move up to the end point on the dotted line.

Alternate Lesson 97 - Practice Words & Phrases

Teaching Tips:

1. Help the children with these practice words and phrases. Have them trace these then practice writing them.
2. Watch formation and spacing.
3. Read and discuss the poem.
4. Additional blank lines may be used for practice phrases, words and so on.

Lessons 98 - Review Cursive

Teaching Tips:

1. Review cursive letters taught to this point.
2. Note those letters in sequence: A, B, C, D, E, F, G, H, I.
3. Review cursive letter formation.

Poem for Lessons 96-100

When Fishes Set Umbrellas Up

"When fishes set umbrellas up
If rain-drops run,
Lizards will want their parasols
To shade them from the sun."

Alternate Lesson 98 - Practice Sentences

Teaching Tips:

1. Help the children with these sentences. Have them trace these then practice writing them.
2. Watch formation and spacing.
3. Read and discuss the poem.
4. Additional blank lines may be used for practice, sentences, phrases, words and so on.

Lesson 98 ✳ Name:

Aa Bb Cc Dd

Ee Ff Gg Hh

Ii Kk Oo Qq Tt

fed fed be be

feed feed feet feet

Horizons Penmanship Grade Two 115

Alternate Lesson 98

Umbrellas keep us dry.

Parasols keep the sun

off of us.

Have you seen a lizard

with a parasol?

Horizons Penmanship Grade Two

Lesson 99 - Poem

Teaching Tips:

1. Introduce new or unfamiliar words: "parasols."
2. Practice the poem.

Poem for Lessons 96-100

When Fishes Set Umbrellas Up

"When fishes set umbrellas up
   If rain-drops run,
   Lizards will want their parasols
   To shade them from the sun."

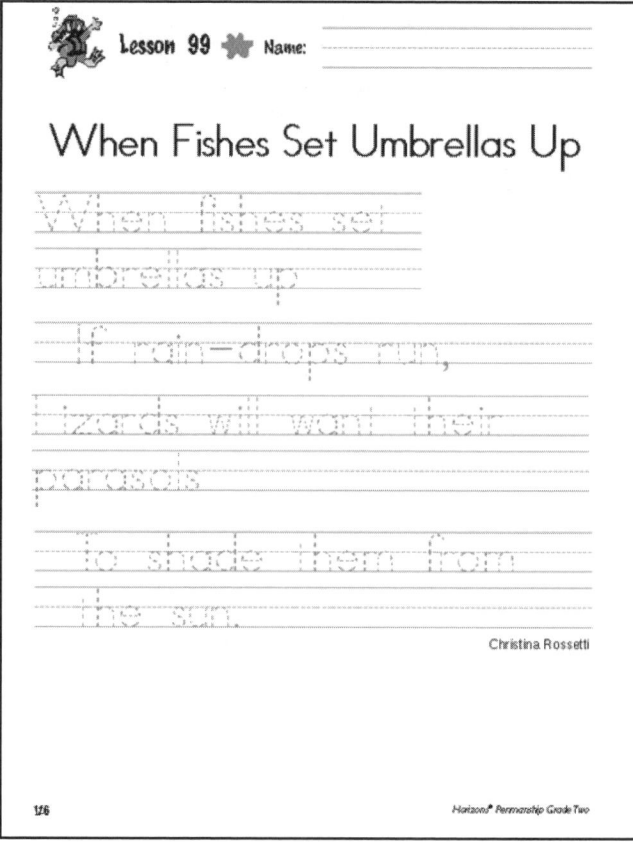

Lesson 100 - Special Page

Teaching Tips:

1. Explain that the children will copy the poem from Lesson 99 onto this special page using their best handwriting skills.
2. Allow the children to practice on the corresponding reproducible practice page from the back of this manual.
3. Complete final copy.
4. Decide how this special page will be used.

Lesson 101 - Introduction to Cursive Letter L, l

Teaching Tips:

1. Quote for the week: from **The Kitten and the Falling Leaves** by William Wordsworth. This very long poem need not be taken in its entirety, but selections may be taken throughout the week.

The Kitten and the Falling Leaves

THAT way look, my Infant, lo!
What a pretty baby-show!
  See the Kitten on the wall,
  Sporting with the leaves that fall,
  Withered leaves—one—two—and three—
  From the lofty elder-tree!
  Through the calm and frosty air
  Of this morning bright and fair,
Eddying round and round they sink
Softly, slowly: one might think,   10
From the motions that are made,
Every little leaf conveyed
Sylph or Faery hither tending,—
To this lower world descending,
Each invisible and mute,
In his wavering parachute.
——But the Kitten, how she starts,
Crouches, stretches, paws and darts!
First at one and then its fellow
Just as light and just as yellow;   20
There are many now—now one—
Now they stop and there are none.
What intenseness of desire
In her upward eye of fire!
With a tiger-leap half-way
Now she meets the coming prey,
Lets it go as fast and then
Has it in her power again:
Now she works with three or four,
Like an Indian conjurer;   30
Quick as he in feats of art,
Far beyond in joy of heart.
Were her antics played in the eye
Of a thousand standers-by,

Clapping hands with shout and stare,
What would little Tabby care
For the plaudits of the crowd?
Over happy to be proud,
Over wealthy in the treasure
Of her own exceeding pleasure!   40
'Tis a pretty baby-treat;
Nor, I deem, for me unmeet;
Here, for neither Babe nor me,
Other play-mate can I see.
Of the countless living things,
That with stir of feet and wings
(In the sun or under shade,
Upon bough or grassy blade)
And with busy revellings,
Chirp and song and murmurings,   50
Made this orchard's narrow space,
And this vale so blithe a place;
Multitudes are swept away
Never more to breathe the day:
Some are sleeping; some in bands
Travelled into distant lands;
Others slunk to moor and wood,
Far from human neighbourhood;
And, among the Kinds that keep
With us closer fellowship,   60
With us openly abide,

All have laid their mirth aside.
Where is he that giddy Sprite,
Blue-cap, with his colours bright,
Who was blest as bird could be,
Feeding in the apple-tree;
Made such wanton spoil and rout,
Turning blossoms inside out;
Hung—head pointing towards the ground—
Fluttered, perched, into a round   70
Bound himself and then unbound;
Lithest, gaudiest Harlequin!
Prettiest Tumbler ever seen!
Light of heart and light of limb;
What is now become of Him?
Lambs, that through the mountains went
Frisking, bleating merriment,
When the year was in its prime,
They are sobered by this time.
If you look to vale or hill,   80
If you listen, all is still,
Save a little neighbouring rill,
That from out the rocky ground
Strikes a solitary sound.
Vainly glitter hill and plain,
And the air is calm in vain;
Vainly Morning spreads the lure
Of a sky serene and pure;
Creature none can she decoy
Into open sign of joy: 90
Is it that they have a fear
Of the dreary season near?
Or that other pleasures be
Sweeter even than gaiety?
Yet, whate'er enjoyments dwell
In the impenetrable cell
Of the silent heart which Nature
Furnishes to every creature;
Whatsoe'er we feel and know
Too sedate for outward show,   100
Such a light of gladness breaks,
Pretty Kitten! from thy freaks,—
Spreads with such a living grace
O'er my little Dora's face;
Yes, the sight so stirs and charms
Thee, Baby, laughing in my arms,
That almost I could repine
That your transports are not mine,
That I do not wholly fare
Even as ye do, thoughtless pair!   110
And I will have my careless season

Spite of melancholy reason,
Will walk through life in such a way
That, when time brings on decay,
Now and then I may possess
Hours of perfect gladsomeness.
—Pleased by any random toy;
By a kitten's busy joy,
Or an infant's laughing eye
Sharing in the ecstasy;   120
I would fare like that or this,
Find my wisdom in my bliss;
Keep the sprightly soul awake,
And have faculties to take,
Even from things by sorrow wrought,
Matter for a jocund thought,
Spite of care and spite of grief,
To gambol with Life's falling Leaf.

2. Introduce the cursive letter: **Ll**

3. The capital "L" is a letter of "loops." It begins on the dotted line, curves up to the top line where it loops around and down to the bottom line. As it touches the bottom line it makes a small loop up, around, then curves slightly below the bottom line and back up to end at the bottom line.

4. The small "l" is a tall loop that begins like the small "b, f, h and k" with an upstroke from bottom to top and a loop around and back down to the bottom. When it touches the bottom line it curves back up to the end point at the dotted line.

Poem for Lessons 101-106

"See the Kitten on the wall,
  Sporting with the leaves that fall,
  Withered leaves – one – two – and three –
  From the lofty elder-tree!
  Through the calm and frosty air
  Of this morning bright and fair."

118

Alternate Lesson 101 - Practice Phrases

Teaching Tips:

1. Help the children with these phrases. Have them trace these then practice writing them.

2. Watch formation and spacing.

3. Read and discuss the poem.

4. Additional blank lines may be used for practice phrases, words and so on.

Alternate Lesson 101

withered leaves

cider trees

frosty air

Lesson 102 - Introduction to Cursive Letter P, p

Teaching Tips:

1. Introduce the cursive letter: **Pp**.

2. The capital "P" begins like the capital "B" with an upstroke from the dotted line to the top line, followed by a down stroke which is traced back to the top and around. It curves around and back to meet the down stroke at the dotted line.

3. The small "p" begins like the small "i" with an upstroke from the bottom line to the dotted line. It then continues with a down stroke that extends one space below the bottom line. It loops back around and up to the dotted line where it curves around, down and back to the bottom line. It ends with an upstroke that goes to the dotted line.

Alternate Lesson 102 - Practice Phrases

Teaching Tips:

1. Help the children with these phrases. Have them trace these then practice writing them.

2. Watch formation and spacing.

3. Read and discuss the poem.

4. Additional blank lines may be used for practice phrases, words and so on.

P P P P

P p p p

P

p

pat pat

apple apple

190   Horizons Penmanship Grade Two

Alternate Lesson 102

See the kitten

sporting with leaves

through the calm and

frosty air

Horizons Penmanship Grade Two

Lesson 103 - Introduction to Cursive Letter N, n

Teaching Tips:

1. Introduce the cursive letter: **Nn**.

2. The capital "N" begins like the "H" and the "K" with a stroke that begins on the top line and hooks slightly into a down stroke. When the down stroke reaches the bottom line, it moves back up again and begins to form an arch at the dotted line. The arch moves up and around midway between the dotted and top lines, then curves down to the bottom line and back up to the end point at the dotted line.

3. The small "n" begins at the bottom line with an upstroke that curves slightly around into a small down stroke that extends to the bottom line. It then moves up to make an arch at the dotted line, around, down to the bottom line and up to the end point at the dotted line.

4. Note the word "kitten" and have the children find it in the quote.

Poem for Lessons 101-106

"See the Kitten on the wall,
  Sporting with the leaves that fall,
  Withered leaves – one – two – and three –
  From the lofty elder-tree!
  Through the calm and frosty air
  Of this morning bright and fair."

Alternate Lesson 103 - Practice Phrases

Teaching Tips:

1. Help the children with these phrases. Have them trace these then practice writing them.

2. Watch formation and spacing.

3. Read and discuss the poem.

4. Additional blank lines may be used for practice phrases, words and so on.

one, two, and three

Of the morning bright

and fair

Lesson 104 - Poem

Teaching Tips:

1. Introduce new or unfamiliar words: "sporting," "withered," "elder tree."
2. Practice the poem.

Poem for Lessons 101-106

"See the Kitten on the wall,
  Sporting with the leaves that fall,
  Withered leaves – one – two – and three –
  From the lofty elder-tree!
  Through the calm and frosty air
  Of this morning bright and fair."

Lesson 105: Special Page

Teaching Tips:

1. Explain that the children will copy the poem from Lesson 104 onto this special page using their best handwriting skills.
2. Allow the children to practice on the corresponding reproducible practice page from the back of this manual.
3. Complete final copy allowing extra time because of the length.
4. Decide how this special page will be used.

Lesson 106 - Introduction to Cursive Letter M, m

Teaching Tips:

1. Quote for the week: from **The Tiger** by William Blake. Note that the part they will write appears at both the beginning and the ending of the poem.

The Tiger

Tiger! Tiger! burning bright,
In the forests of the night;
What immortal band or eye,
Could frame thy fearful symmetry?

 In what distant deeps or skies.
Burnt the fire of thine eyes?
On what wings dare he aspire?
What the hand, dare sieze the fire?

And what shoulder, & what art,
Could twist the sinews of thy heart?
And when thy heart began to beat,
What dread hand? & what dread feet?

What the hammer? what the chain,
In what furnace was thy brain?
What the anvil? what dread grasp,
Dare its deadly terrors clasp!

When the stars threw down their spears
And water'd heaven with their tears:
Did he smile his work to see?
Did he who made the Lamb make thee?

Tiger! Tiger! burning bright,
In the forests of the night:
What immortal hand or eye,
Dare frame thy fearful symmetry?

2. Introduce the cursive letter: **Mm**.
3. The capital "M" begins like the capital "N" but adds an additional arch that is not quite as tall as the first one.
4. The small "m" begins like the small "n" but adds an additional arch that also touches the dotted line.

Poem for Lessons 106-110

The Tiger

"Tiger! Tiger! burning bright,
 In the forests of the night;
 What immortal band or eye,
 Could frame thy fearful symmetry?"

Alternate Lesson 106 – Practice Phrases

Teaching Tips:

1. Help the children with these phrases. Have them trace these then practice writing them.

2. Watch formation and spacing.

3. Read and discuss the poem.

4. Additional blank lines may be used for practice phrases, words and so on.

tiger   tiger

burning   bright

forests   of   the   night

Horizons Penmanship Grade Two

Lesson 107 - Introduction to Cursive Letter R, r

Teaching Tips:

1. Read additional stanzas of the poem. Ask children to share their impressions of tigers if they have seen them in the zoo or wild life park.

2. Introduce the cursive letter: **Rr**.

3. The capital "R" begins like the capital "P." After closing the curve, it continues on down to curve at the bottom line before moving up to the end point at the dotted line.

4. The small "r" begins like the small "i" with a short upstroke from the bottom line to the dotted line. It then makes a slight angled line down before curving down to the bottom line and back up to the end point at the dotted line.

Alternate Lesson 107 - Practice Phrases

Teaching Tips:

1. Help the children with these phrases. Have them trace these then practice writing them.

2. Watch formation and spacing.

3. Read and discuss the poem.

4. Additional blank lines may be used for practice phrases, words and so on.

Lesson 108 - Practice Cursive Words

Teaching Tips:

1. Cursive word practice. Write the words for today in manuscript on the board and have the children compare them.

2. Observe spacing, formation and slant of letters.

Poem for Lessons 106-110

The Tiger

"Tiger! Tiger! burning bright,
 In the forests of the night;
 What immortal band or eye,
 Could frame thy fearful symmetry?"

Alternate Lesson 108 - Practice Words

Teaching Tips:

1. Help the children with these words. Have them trace these then practice writing them.

2. Watch formation and spacing.

3. Read and discuss the poem.

4. Additional blank lines may be used for practice phrases, words and so on.

Lesson 108 Name:

fearful

night

bright

hand

could

Alternate Lesson 108

fearful

night

bright

hand

could

Lesson 109 - Poem

Teaching Tips:

1. Introduce any new or unfamiliar words: "symmetry."

2. Practice the poem.

Poem for Lessons 106-110

The Tiger

"Tiger! Tiger! burning bright,
 In the forests of the night;
 What immortal band or eye,
 Could frame thy fearful symmetry?"

Lesson 110 - Special Page

Teaching Tips:

1. Explain that the children will copy the poem from Lesson 109 onto this special page using their best handwriting skills.

4. Allow the children to practice on the corresponding reproducible practice page at the back of this manual.

5. Complete final copy allowing extra time because of the length.

6. Decide how this special page will be used.

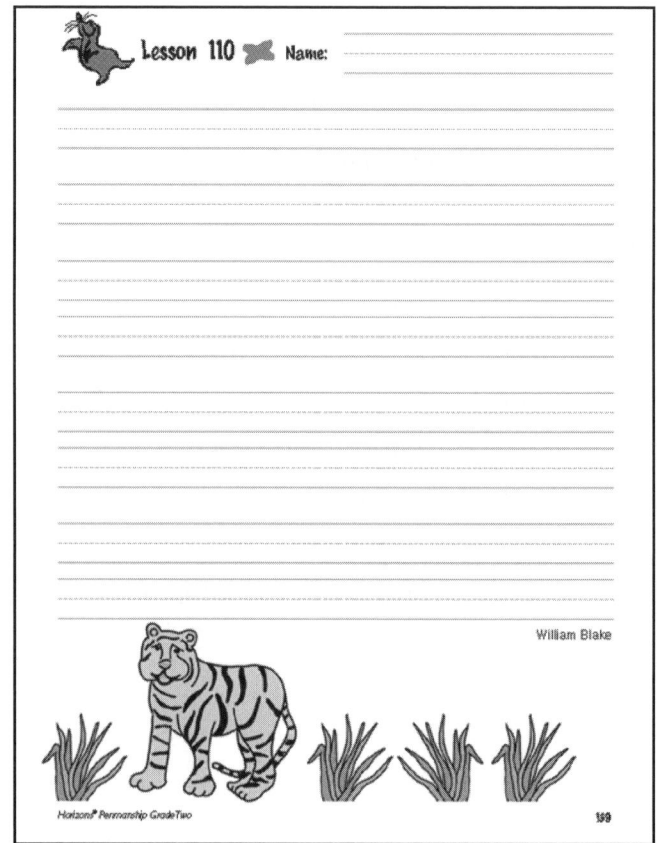

Lesson 111 - Introduction to Cursive Letter U, u

Teaching Tips:

1. Quote for the week: **The Eagle** by Alfred Lord Tennyson. Children write the entire poem.

2. Introduce the cursive letter: **Uu**.

3. The capital "U" begins with the same stroke as the "H, K, M and N." When it reaches the bottom line it curves around and back up to the top line. It then retraces the same line back down and curves up to the end point at the dotted line.

4. The small "u" of three connected upstrokes. It begins on the bottom line, moves up to the dotted line, curves down, around and up to the dotted line again, then moves back down, around and up to the end point at the dotted line.

Lesson 111   Name:

Horizons Penmanship Grade Two   141

Poem for Lessons 111-115

The Eagle

"He clasps the crag with crooked hands;
Close to the sun in lonely lands,
Ringed with azure world, he stands
The wrinkled sea beneath him crawls;
He watches from his mountain walls,
And like a thunderbolt he falls."

Alternate Lesson 111 - Practice Phrases

Teaching Tips:

1. Help the children with these phrases. Have them trace these then practice writing them.
2. Watch formation and spacing.
3. Read and discuss the poem.
4. Additional blank lines may be used for practice phrases, words and so on.

Alternate Lesson 111

crooked hands

clasps the crag

close to the sun

Lesson 112: Introduction to Cursive Letter S, s

Teaching Tips:

1. Read the poem and discuss some of the visual images of the eagle: clasping the cliff with crooked hands; diving like a thunderbolt for his prey.

2. Introduce the cursive letter: **Ss**.

3. The capital "S" begins like the small "l, b, f, h and k" with an upstroke from bottom to top and a loop around and back. It curves back across the upstroke and around to the bottom line, then curves back around and up to the dotted line ending in a "smile" like the final strokes of the "I, F, T."

4. The small "s" begins like the small "i and r" with a short upstroke from the bottom line to the dotted line. It curves down and back to the original upstroke line, then up and out in a short line that ends at the dotted line (like the small "p").

Poem for Lessons 111-115

The Eagle

"He clasps the crag with crooked hands;
Close to the sun in lonely lands,
Ringed with azure world, he stands
The wrinkled sea beneath him crawls;
He watches from his mountain walls,
And like a thunderbolt he falls."

Alternate Lesson 112 - Practice Phrases

Teaching Tips:

1. Help the children with these phrases. Have them trace these then practice writing them.

2. Watch formation and spacing.

3. Read and discuss the poem.

4. Additional blank lines may be used for practice phrases, words and so on.

Alternate Lesson 112

azure world

wrinkled sea

ringed the world

Lesson 113 - Introduction to Cursive Letter W, w

Teaching Tips:

1. Ask the children what they think the phrase "wrinkled sea" refers to in the poem. If children have never observed waves from a distance, try to find a picture that will give them the visual effect.

2. Introduce the cursive letter: **Ww**.

3. The capital "W" is formed like the capital "U," but the final line curves up to the top line.

4. The small "w" is formed like the small "u," with an added line that curves slightly along the dotted line.

Poem for Lessons 111-115

The Eagle

"He clasps the crag with crooked hands;
Close to the sun in lonely lands,
Ringed with azure world, he stands
The wrinkled sea beneath him crawls;
He watches from his mountain walls,
And like a thunderbolt he falls."

Alternate Lesson 113 - Practice Words & Phrases

Teaching Tips:

1. Help the children with these words and phrases. Have them trace these then practice writing them.

2. Watch formation and spacing.

3. Read and discuss the poem.

4. Additional blank lines may be used for practice phrases, words and so on.

W W W W

W w W w

W

w

with with

world world

Alternate Lesson 113

mountain walls,

thunderbolt

He watches and falls

Lesson 114 - Poem

Teaching Tips:

1. Introduce any new or unfamiliar words: "crag," "azure."

2. Practice the poem.

Poem for Lessons 111-115

The Eagle

"He clasps the crag with crooked hands;
Close to the sun in lonely lands,
Ringed with azure world, he stands
The wrinkled sea beneath him crawls;
He watches from his mountain walls,
And like a thunderbolt he falls."

Lesson 114   Name:
The Eagle

He clasps the crag with
crooked hands,
Close to the sun in
lonely lands,
Ringed with azure world,
he stands
The wrinkled sea beneath
him crawls;
He watches from his
mountain walls,
And like a thunderbolt
he falls.

Alfred, Lord Tennyson

144   Horizons Penmanship Grade Two

Lesson 115 - Special Page

Teaching Tips:

1. Explain that the children will copy the poem from Lesson 114 onto this special page using their best handwriting skills.

2. Allow the children to practice on the corresponding reproducible practice page from the back of this manual.

3. Complete final copy allowing extra time because of the length.

4. Decide how this special page will be used.

Lesson 115   Name:
The Eagle

Alfred, Lord Tennyson

Horizons Penmanship Grade Two   145

Lesson 116 - Introduction to Cursive Letter Y, y

Teaching Tips:

1. Quote for the week: from **A Bird Came Down the Walk** by Emily Dickinson.

   A Bird Came Down the Walk

   A bird came down the walk:
   He did not know I saw;
   He bit an angle-worm in halves
   And ate the fellow, raw.

   And then he drank a dew
   From a convenient grass,
   And then hopped sidewise to the wall
   To let a beetle pass.

   He glanced with rapid eyes
   That hurried all abroad,—
   They looked like frightened beads,
   I thought;He stirred his velvet head

   Like one in danger; cautious,
   I offered him a crumb,
   And he unrolled his feathers
   And rowed him softer home

   Than oars divide the ocean,
   Too silver for a seam,
   Or butterflies, off banks of noon,
   Leap, splashless, as they swim.

2. Introduce the cursive letter: **Yy**.
3. The capital "Y" begins like the capital "U." After making the "U" shape, the downward line continues on into the

space below the bottom line, then loops back and up to the bottom line.

4. The small "y" begins with an upstroke from the bottom line to the dotted line which curves up, over and back down to the bottom line where is begins a second upstroke to the dotted line. The line then moves down one space below the bottom line, loops back, around, up across the bottom line to the end point at the dotted line.

Poem for Lessons 116-120

"A bird came down the walk:
 He did not know I saw;
 He bit an angle-worm in halves
 And ate the fellow, raw.

Alternate Lesson 116 – Practice Words & Phrases

Teaching Tips:

1. Help the children with these words and phrases. Have them trace these then practice writing them.

2. Watch formation and spacing.

3. Read and discuss the poem.

4. Additional blank lines may be used for practice phrases, words and so on.

A Bird Came Down the

Walk

Emily

Dickinson

Lesson 117 - Introduction to Cursive Letter V, v

Teaching Tips:

1. Read additional stanzas of the poem. Ask how many children have seen birds digging worms in the garden or yard.

2. Introduce the cursive letter: **Vv.**

3. The capital "V" Begins like the capital "U" and "W." After curving around the bottom line if moves up to the top line where it ends in a slight curve.

4. The small "v" begins with an upstroke from the bottom line to the dotted line which curves up, over and back down to the bottom line, then moves around and back to the dotted line where it ends with a slight curve (like the "w").

Poem for Lessons 116-120

"A bird came down the walk:
 He did not know I saw;
 He bit an angle-worm in halves
 And ate the fellow, raw."

Alternate Lesson 117 - Practice Words

Teaching Tips:

1. Help the children with these words. Have them trace these then practice writing them.

2. Watch formation and spacing.

3. Read and discuss the poem.

4. Additional blank lines may be used for practice phrases, words and so on.

V v V v

V v V v

v

v

very very

148

Horizons® Penmanship Grade Two

Alternate Lesson 117

halves

fellow

worm

Horizons® Penmanship Grade Two

Lesson 118 - Practice Sentences

Teaching Tips:

1. Read entire poem. Emphasize the quote the children will write, this time all in cursive.
2. The children will be writing sentences. Read the sentences with the children to make sure they understand them.
3. Note the spacing between words and sentences.
4. Have the children trace, then copy each sentence.

Poem for Lessons 116-120

"A bird came down the walk:
 He did not know I saw;
 He bit an angle-worm in halves
 And ate the fellow, raw."

Alternate Lesson 118 - Practice Sentences

Teaching Tips:

1. Help the children with these sentences. Have them trace these then practice writing them.
2. Watch formation and spacing.
3. Read and discuss the poem.
4. Additional blank lines may be used for practice sentences, phrases, words and so on.

A bird came down.

He did not know I

saw. He bit a worm

in halves. He ate

the fellow, raw.

Alternate Lesson 118

A bird came down.

He did not know I saw.

He bit a worm in halves.

He ate the fellow, raw.

Lesson 119 - Poem

Teaching Tips:

1. Introduce new or unfamiliar words. Note punctuation used.
2. Practice the poem.

Poem for Lessons 116-120

"A bird came down the walk:
 He did not know I saw;
 He bit an angle-worm in halves
 And ate the fellow, raw.

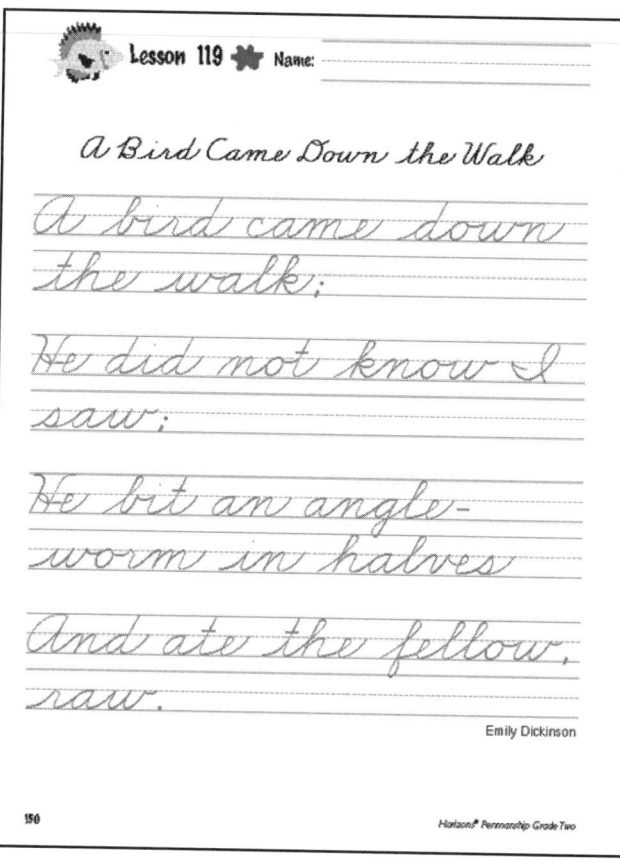

Alternate Lesson 119 - Practice Poem

Teaching Tips:

1. Help the children with this poem. Have them trace this then practice writing it.
2. Watch formation and spacing.
3. Read and discuss the poem.
4. Practice writing on a separate sheet of paper.

Lesson 120 - Special Page

Teaching Tips:

1. Explain that the children will copy the poem from Lesson 119 onto this special page using their best handwriting skills.

2. Allow the children to practice on the corresponding reproducible practice page from the back of this manual.

3. Complete the final copy. If children are having difficulty with cursive, use the manuscript version in the Teacher's Guide.

4. Decide how this special page will be used.

Poem for Lessons 116-120

"A bird came down the walk:
  He did not know I saw;
  He bit an angle-worm in halves
  And ate the fellow, raw."

A Bird Came Down the Walk

Emily Dickinson

Horizons Penmanship Grade Two   151

Lesson 121 – Introduction to Cursive Letter J, j

Teaching Tips:

1. Quote for the week: from **Written in March** by William Wordsworth.

"Written in March"

The cock is crowing,
The stream is flowing,
The small birds twitter,
The lake doth glitter,
The green field sleeps in the sun;
　The oldest and youngest
　Are at work with the strongest;
　The cattle are grazing,
　Their heads never raising;
There are forty feeding like one!　　　10
　Like an army defeated
　The snow hath retreated,
　And now doth fare ill
　On the top of the bare hill;
The ploughboy is whooping—anon—anon:
　There's joy in the mountains;
　There's life in the fountains;
　Small clouds are sailing,
　Blue sky prevailing;
The rain is over and gone!　　　20

2. Introduce the cursive letter: **Jj**.

3. The capital "J" consists of two loops. It begins at the bottom line and loops back, around and up to the top line (like the "I"). It then moves with a long down stroke all the way down one space below the bottom line, loops back around and up crossing the bottom line and continuing to the end point at the dotted line.

4. The small "j" is a two-stroke letter. The first stroke begins with a short upstroke from the bottom line to the dotted line. It continues down to one space below the bottom line, loops back around and up across the bottom line to the end point at the dotted line. The second stroke is the dot placed above the letter in the middle of the upper space.

Poem for Lessons 121-125

Written in March

"The cock is crowing,
　The stream is flowing,
　The small birds twitter,
　The lake doth glitter,
　The green field sleeps in the sun;

Alternate Lesson 121 - Practice Words & Phrases

Teaching Tips:

1. Help the children with these words and phrases. Have them trace these then practice writing them.

2. Watch formation and spacing.

3. Read and discuss the poem.

4. Additional blank lines may be used for practice phrases, words and so on.

growing

flowing

green field sleeps

written

Horizons Penmanship Grade Two

Lesson 122 - Introduction to Cursive Letter X, x

Teaching Tips:

1. Read the entire poem with the children. If the children have experienced different seasons of the year, ask them to compare their own reaction to the change from winter to spring with that in the poem.

2. Introduce the cursive letter: **Xx.**

3. The capital "X" is a two-stroke letter. The first stroke is the same stroke as the first stroke of the "H" and "K." The second stroke begins at the top line, moves straight into touch the first stroke at the dotted line, then curves down and around at the bottom line ending about mid space.

4. The small "x" is also a two-stroke letter. The first stroke begins at the bottom line, curves up to the dotted line, then around, down to the bottom line, then up to the end point at the dotted line. The second stroke is a slant cross line from the dotted line back across the first stroke to the bottom line.

Poem for Lessons 121-125

Written in March

"The cock is crowing,
The stream is flowing,
The small birds twitter,
The lake doth glitter,
The green field sleeps in the sun;"

Alternate Lesson 122 - Practice Words

Teaching Tips:

1. Help the children with these words. Have them trace these then practice writing them.

2. Watch formation and spacing.

3. Read and discuss the poem.

4. Additional blank lines may be used for practice phrases, words and so on.

twitter

glitter

stream

March

Lesson 123 - Sentence Practice

Teaching Tips:

1. The children will be writing sentences. Read the sentences with the children to make sure they understand them.
2. Note the formation, slant and spacing between words and sentences.

Poem for Lessons 121-125

Written in March

"The cock is crowing,
The stream is flowing,
The small birds twitter,
The lake doth glitter,
The green field sleeps in the sun;"

Alternate Lesson 123 - Sentence Practice

Teaching Tips:

1. Help the children with these sentences. Have them trace these then practice writing them.
2. Watch formation and spacing.
3. Read and discuss the poem.
4. Additional blank lines may be used for practice sentences, phrases, words and so on.

The cock is crowing.

The stream is flowing.

The small birds

twitter. The lake doth

glitter. The green field

sleeps in the sun.

Horizons® Penmanship Grade Two 155

Alternate Lesson 123

The cock is crowing. The

stream is flowing. The

small birds twitter. The

lake doth glitter. The green

field sleeps in the sun.

Horizons® Penmanship Grade Two

Lesson 124 - Poem

Teaching Tips:

1. Introduce any new or unfamiliar words: "twitter."
2. Practice the poem.
3. Practice writing the poem on a separate sheet of paper.

Poem for Lessons 121-125

Written in March

"The cock is crowing,
The stream is flowing,
The small birds twitter,
The lake doth glitter,
The green field sleeps in the sun;"

Alternate Lesson 124 - Practice Poem

Teaching Tips:

1. Help the children with this poem. Have them trace this then practice writing it.
2. Watch formation and spacing.
3. Read and discuss the poem.
4. Practice writing the poem on a separate sheet of paper.

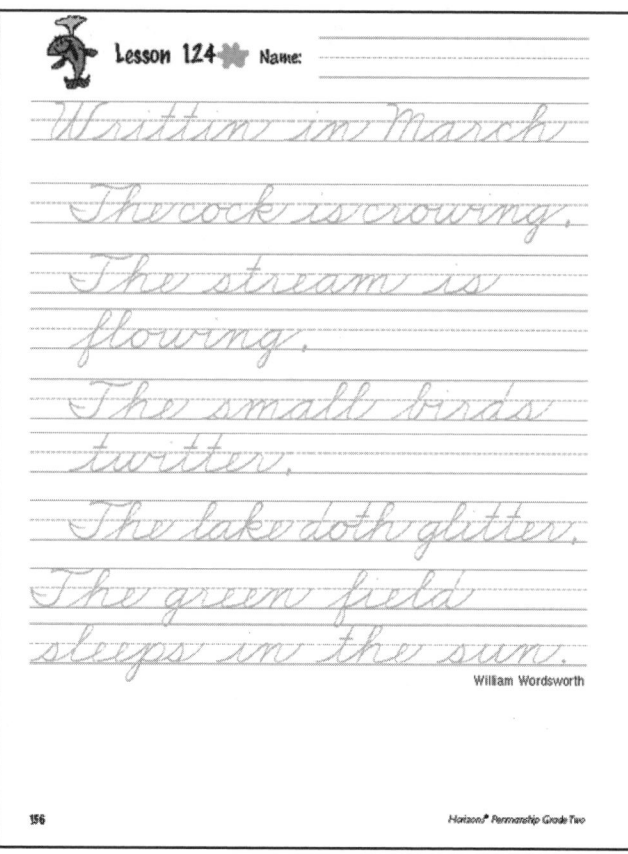

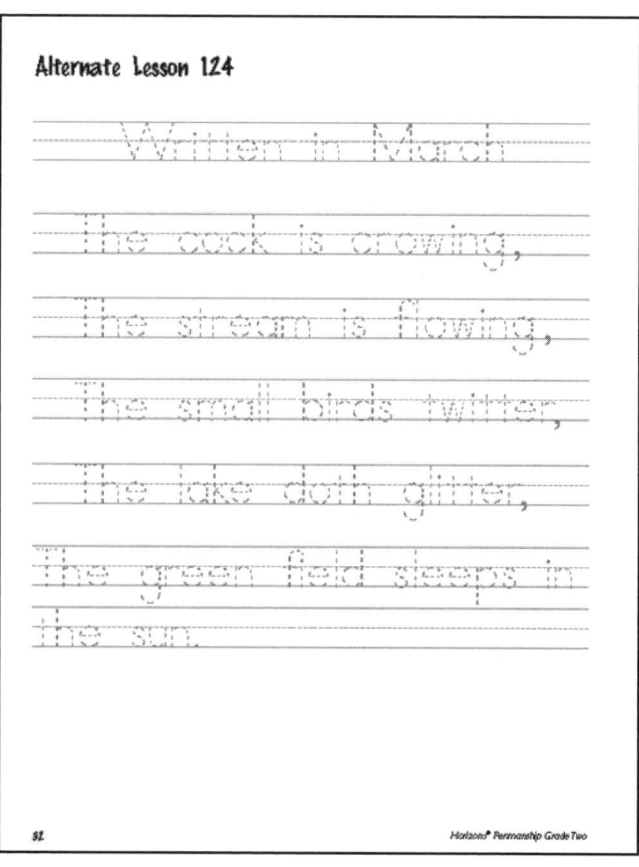

Lesson 125 - Special Page

Teaching Tips:

1. Explain that the children will copy the poem from Lesson 124 onto this special page using their best handwriting skills.

2. Allow the children to practice on the corresponding reproducible practice page from the back of this manual.

3. Complete the final copy. If children are having difficulty with cursive, use the manuscript version in the Teacher's Guide.

4. Decide how this special page will be used.

Poem for Lessons 121-125

Written in March

"The cock is crowing,
The stream is flowing,
The small birds twitter,
The lake doth glitter,
The green field sleeps in the sun;"

Lesson 126 - Introduction to Cursive Letter Z, z

Teaching Tips:

1. Quote for the week: from **Spring Morning** by A. A. Milne.

"Spring Morning"

Where am I going? I don't quite know.
Down to the stream where the king-cups grow—
Up on the hill where the pine-trees blow—
Anywhere, anywhere. *I* don't know.

Where am I going? The clouds sail by,
Little ones, baby ones, over the sky.
Where am I going? The shadows pass,
Little ones, baby ones, over the grass.

If you were a cloud and sailed up there,
You'd sail on water as blue as air,
And you'd see me here in the fields and say:
"Doesn't the sky look green today?"

Where am I going? The high rooks call:
"It's awful fun to be born at all."
Where am I going? The ring-doves coo:
"We do have beautiful things to do."

If you were a bird and lived on high,
You'd lean on the wind when the wind came by,
You'd say to the wind when it took you away:
"That's where I wanted to go today!"

Where am I going? I don't quite know.
What does it matter where people go?
Down to the wood where the blue-bells grow—
Anywhere, anywhere, *I* don't know.

2. This is the third time a stanza of the poem is used this year. Review the poem with the children.

3. Introduce the cursive letter: **Zz**.

4. The capital "Z" begins with the same stroke as the letter "H." When it reaches the bottom line, it makes just a slight move up then curves down a space below the bottom line, loops back around and up across the bottom line to the end point at the dotted line.

5. The small "z" begins with an upstroke from the bottom line to the dotted line, curves over and down to the bottom line, then around again to a space below the bottom line, loops back around and up across the bottom line to the end point at the dotted line.

Poem for Lessons 126-130

"If you were a bird and lived on high,
  You'd lean on the wind when the wind came by,
  You'd say to the wind when it took you away:
  "That's where I wanted to go today!"

Alternate Lesson 126 - Practice Words & Punctuation

Teaching Tips:

1. Help the children with these words and punctuation. Have them trace these then practice writing them.

2. Watch formation and spacing.

3. Read and discuss the poem.

4. Additional blank lines may be used for practice phrases, words and so on.

you'd

that's

Lesson 127 - Review Cursive Letters

Teaching Tips:

1. Review of all cursive letters.
2. If children are having difficulty with individual letters, provide practice paper for them with models of the letters that still need work.

Poem for Lessons 126-130

"If you were a bird and lived on high,
  You'd lean on the wind when the wind
    came by,
You'd say to the wind when it took you
    away:
"That's where I wanted to go today!"

Aa Bb Cc Dd Ee

Ff Gg Hh Ii Jj

Kk Ll Mm Nn Oo

Pp Qq Rr Ss Tt

Uu Vv Ww Xx Yy Zz

Alternate Lesson 127 - Practice Sentences

Teaching Tips:

1. Note the punctuation marks in these sentences.
2. Practice writing these sentences.
3. Read the sentences with the children.

Alternate Lesson 127

A bird can fly.

Can you fly?

What do you want to

do?

Lesson 128 - Working on Sentences

Teaching Tips:

1. Note the contraction, the punctuation and the quotation marks in these sentences.

2. Read the sentences with the children.

Poem for Lessons 126-130

"If you were a bird and lived on high,
   You'd lean on the wind when the wind
      came by,
   You'd say to the wind when it took you
      away:
"That's where I wanted to go today!"

Alternate Lesson 128 - Practice Sentences

Teaching Tips:

1. Note the contraction, the punctuation and the quotation marks in these sentences.

2. Read the sentences with the children.

Lesson 129 - Poem

Teaching Tips:

1. Read the quote with the children.
2. Practice the poem.

Poem for Lessons 126-130

"If you were a bird and lived on high,
  You'd lean on the wind when the wind
    came by,
  You'd say to the wind when it took you
    away:
"That's where I wanted to go today!"

Alternate Lesson 129 - Practice Poem

Teaching Tips:

1. Read the quote with the children.
2. Practice the poem.

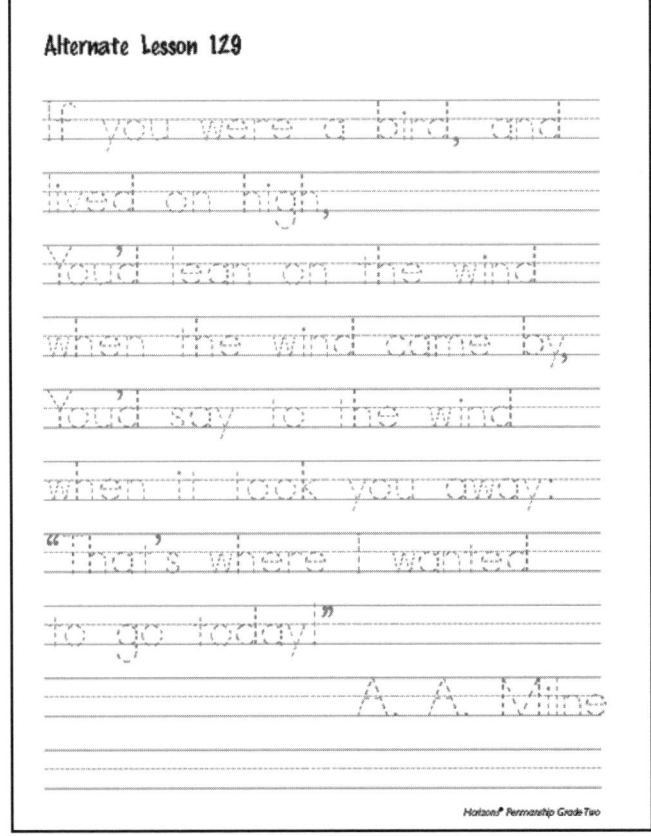

Lesson 130 - Special Page

Teaching Tips:

1. Explain that the children will copy the poem from Lesson 129 onto this special page using their best handwriting skills.

2. Allow the children to practice on the corresponding reproducible practice page from the back of this manual.

3. Complete the final copy allowing additional time because of the length and the differences in punctuation. Manuscript copy provided for those who need it.

4. Decide how this special page will be used.

Poem for Lessons 126-130

"If you were a bird and lived on high,
　You'd lean on the wind when the wind
　　　came by,
　You'd say to the wind when it took you
　　　away:
"That's where I wanted to go today!"

Lessons 130 - 150 Review & Practice Cursive

Review and additional practice for Cursive letters and words. Continue to provide manuscript copies of work to those children who are not yet ready for cursive.

Lessons 131 - 135: Review & Practice

Teaching Tips:

1. Quote for the week: from **"Written in March"** by William Wordsworth.

"Written in March"

The cock is crowing,
The stream is flowing,
The small birds twitter,
The lake doth glitter,
The green field sleeps in the sun;
The oldest and youngest
Are at work with the strongest;
The cattle are grazing,
Their heads never raising;
There are forty feeding like one!   10
Like an army defeated
The snow hath retreated,
And now doth fare ill
On the top of the bare hill;
The ploughboy is whooping—anon—anon:
There's joy in the mountains;
There's life in the fountains;
Small clouds are sailing,
Blue sky prevailing;
The rain is over and gone!   20

TT There's

SS Small

BB Blue

WW William

2. Children should remember this poem from Lessons 121 – 125.

3. See if children can also remember the other quotation which celebrated the rain being "over and gone." (Song of Songs, Lessons 71 – 75).

4. Explain that the children will copy the poem from Lesson 134 onto the special page using their best handwriting skills.

5. Allow the children to practice on a separate sheet of paper.

6. Complete the final copy.

7. Decide how to use the special page.

Poem for Lessons 131-135

"There's joy in the mountains;
There's life in the fountains;
Small clouds are sailing,
Blue sky prevailing;
The rain is over and gone!"

mountains

fountains

sailing

prevailing

There's joy in
the mountains;
There's life in
the fountains;
Small clouds are
sailing,
Blue sky prevailing;
The rain is over
and gone!
Wordsworth

rain is over

joy

life

Wordsworth

Alternate Lessons 131 - 134

Alternate Lesson 131

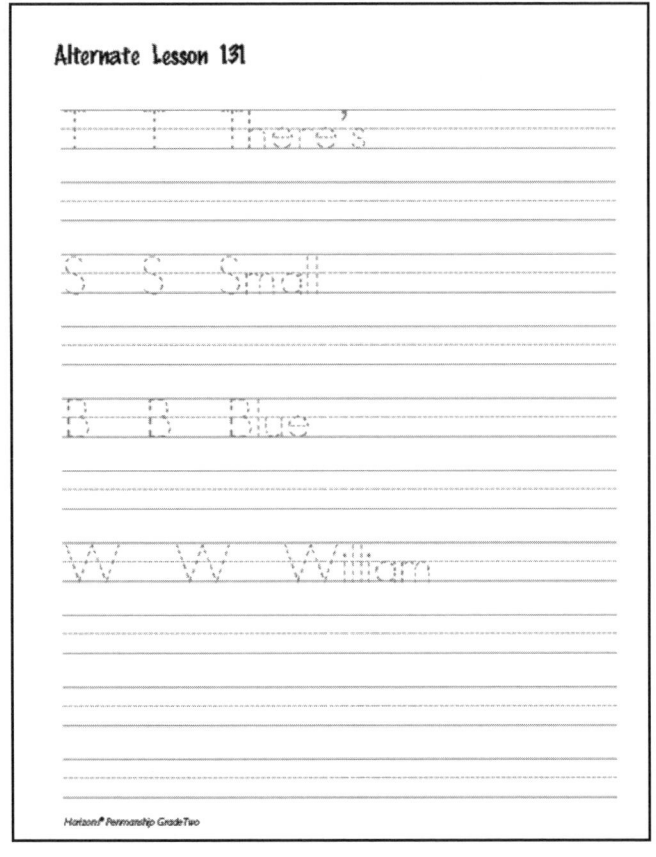

I   I   There's

S   S   Small

B   B   Blue

W   W   William

Alternate Lesson 133

rain is over

joy

life

Wordsworth

Alternate Lesson 132

mountains

fountains

sailing

prevailing

Alternate Lesson 134

There's joy in the
mountains,
There's life in the
fountains,
Small clouds are sailing,
Blue sky prevailing,
The rain is over and
gone !
                Wordsworth

Lessons 136 - 140: Review & Practice

Teaching Tips:

1. Quote for the week: **Psalm 90:2**.
2. Select other verses from Psalm 90 which deal with God's creation.
3. Read through the quote with the children.
4. The children will be writing sentences. Read the sentences with the children to make sure they understand them.
5. Note the spacing between words and sentences.
6. Additional blank lines may be used for practice, for original sentences, for class sentences, for phrases, for rhyming words and so on.
7. Explain that the children will copy the verse from Lesson 139 onto the special page using their best handwriting skills.
8. Allow the children to practice on a separate sheet of paper.
9. Complete the final copy.
10. Decide how to use the special page.

Bible Verse Lessons 136-140

"Lord,
Before the mountains were born or you brought forth the earth and the world, from everlasting to everlasting you are God."
(Psalm 90:2)

Lesson 136   Name:

L L Lord

G G God

P P Psalm

b b born

Horizons Penmanship Grade Two   171

Lesson 137 — Name:

brought forth

the earth

the world

everlasting

171

Horizons Penmanship Grade Two

Lesson 139 — Name:

Lord.

Before the

mountains were

born, you brought

forth the earth and

the world, from

everlasting to

everlasting you are

God.

Psalm 90:2

174

Horizons Penmanship Grade Two

Lesson 138 — Name:

You are God. You

brought forth the

earth. You brought

forth the world.

You are everlasting.

Horizons Penmanship Grade Two

173

Lesson 140 — Name:

Psalm 90:2

Horizons Penmanship Grade Two

175

Alternate Lessons 136 - 139

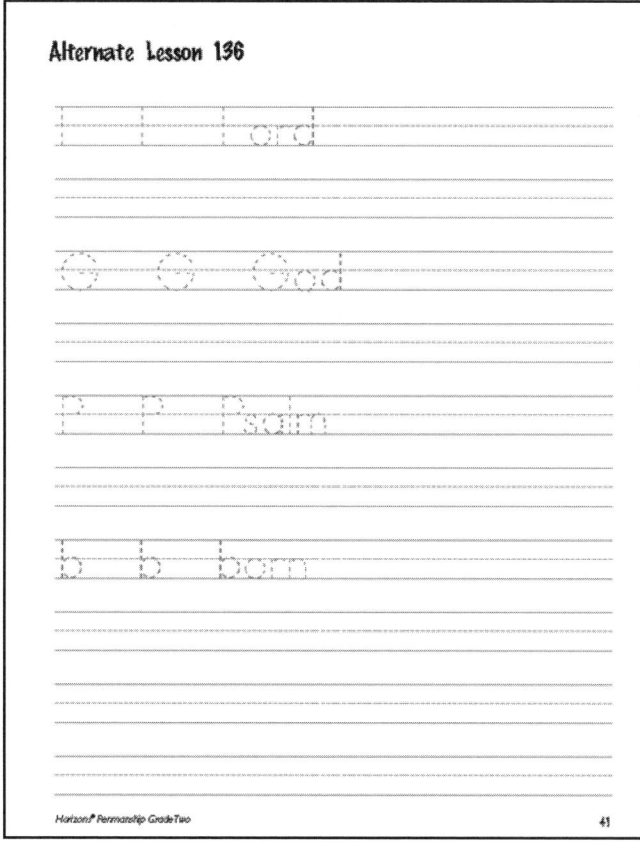

Alternate Lesson 136

L L Lord

G G God

P P Psalm

b b born

Alternate Lesson 137

brought forth

the earth

the world

everlasting

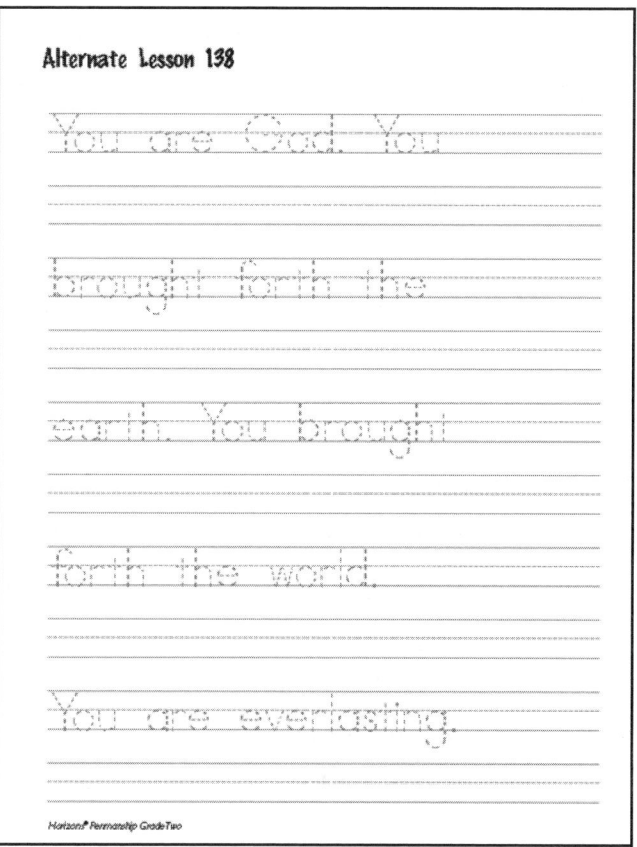

Alternate Lesson 138

You are God. You

brought forth the

earth. You brought

forth the world.

You are everlasting

Alternate Lesson 139

Lord,

Before the mountains

were born or you brought

forth the earth and the

world, from everlasting to

everlasting you are God.

Psalm 90:2

Lessons 141 - 145: Review & Practice

Teaching Tips:

1. Quote for the week: **Psalm 98:7**
2. Read Psalm 98 with the children.
3. Lessons 141-143: check formation of all manuscript and cursive letters.
4. Trace and copy the letters while the teacher observes the position, formation and spacing.
5. Explain that the children will copy the verse from Lesson 144 onto the special page using their best handwriting skills.
6. Allow the children to practice on a separate sheet of paper.
7. Complete the final copy.
8. Decide how to use the special page.

Bible Verse Lessons 141-145

"Let the sea resound and everything in it, the world and all who live in it."
(Psalm 98:7)

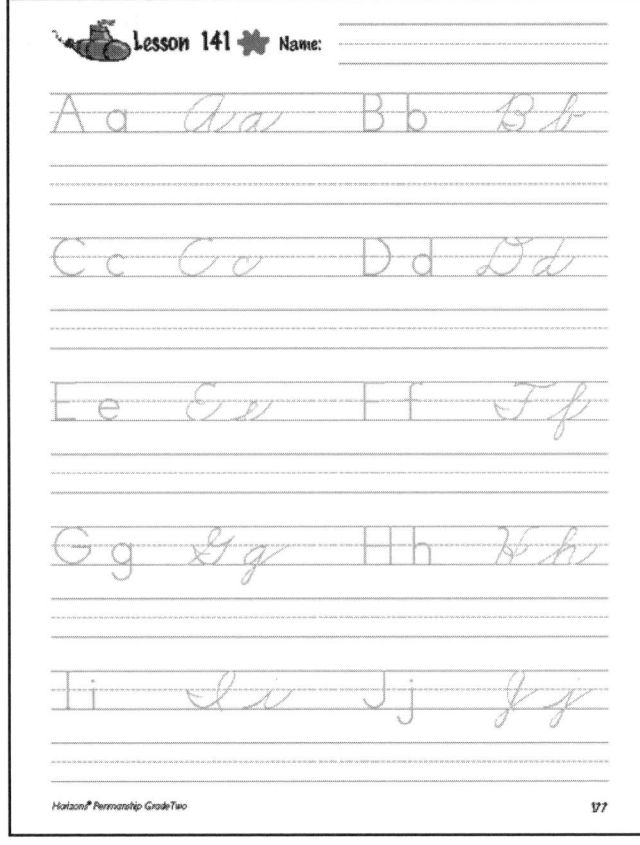

160

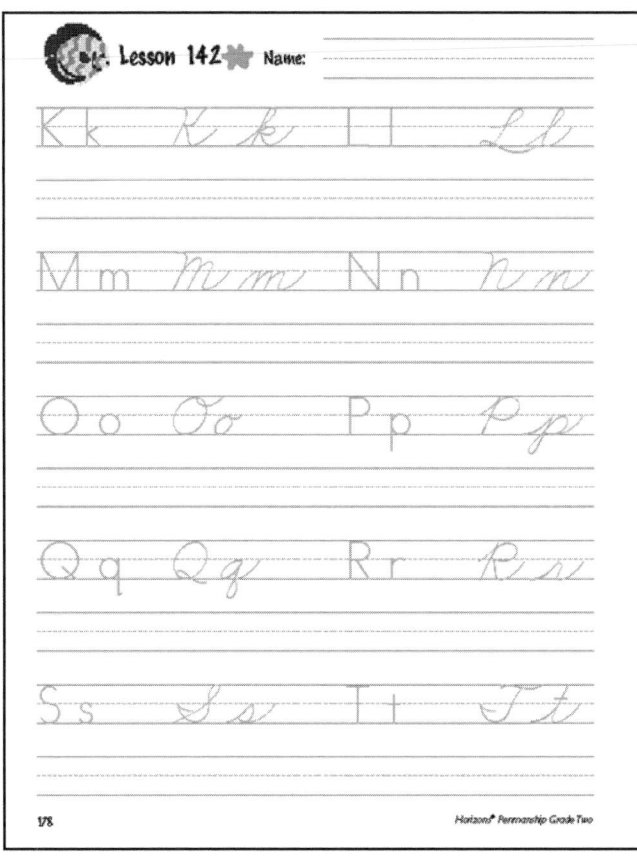

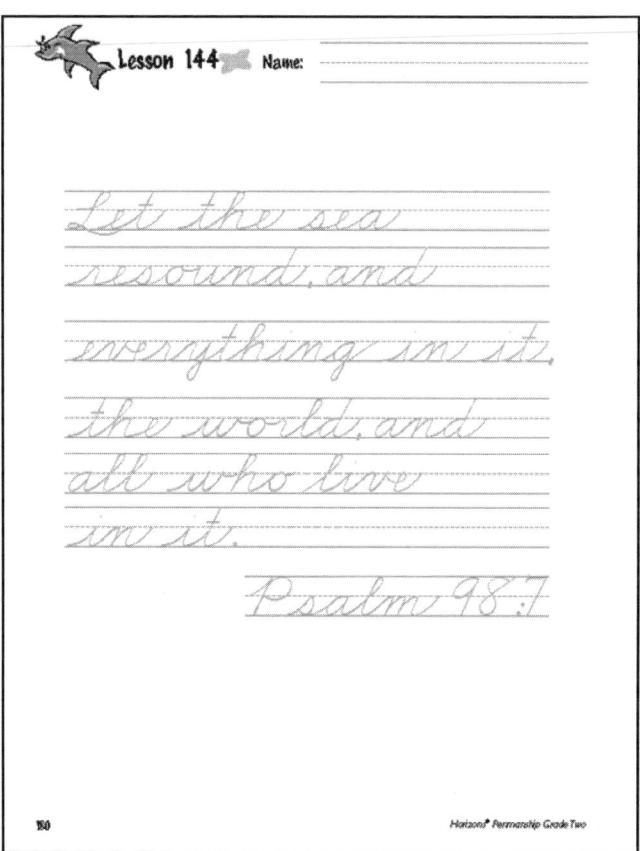

Let the sea
resound, and
everything in it,
the world, and
all who live
in it.
        Psalm 98:7

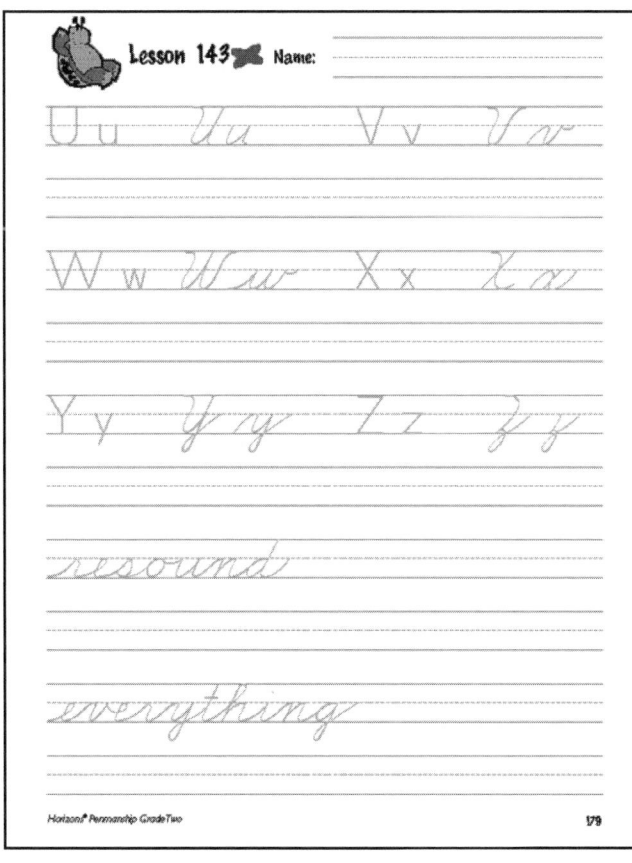

resound

everything

Alternate Lessons 141 - 144

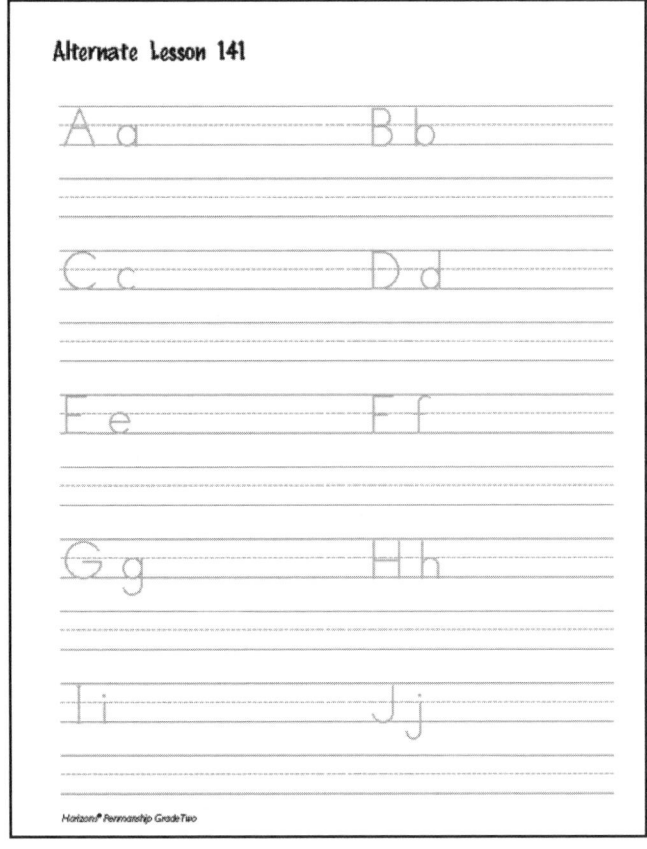

Alternate Lesson 141

Aa   Bb

Cc   Dd

Ee   Ff

Gg   Hh

Ii   Jj

Horizons® Penmanship Grade Two

Alternate Lesson 143

Uu   Vv

Ww   Xx

Yy   Zz

resound

everything

Horizons® Penmanship Grade Two

Alternate Lesson 142

Kk   Ll

Mm   Nn

Oo   Pp

Qq   Rr

Ss   Tt

Horizons® Penmanship Grade Two

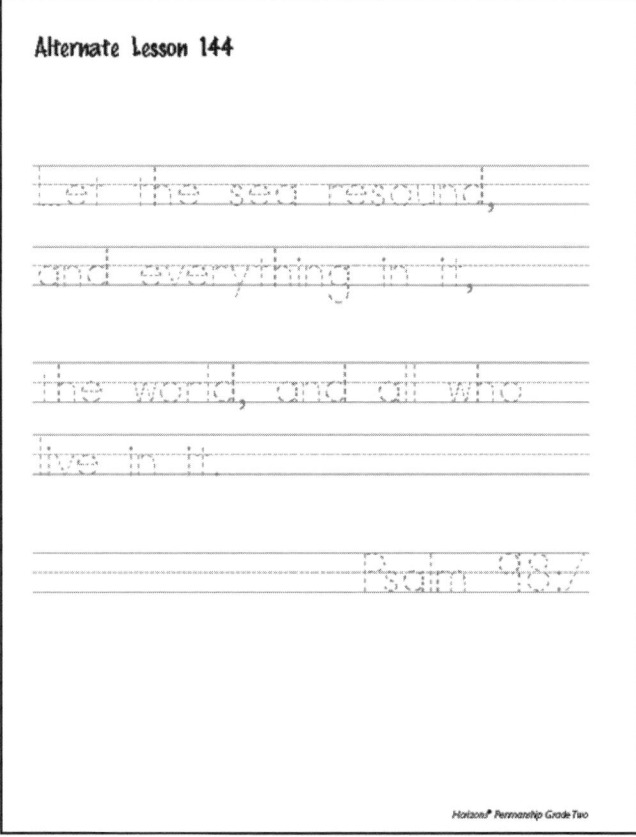

Alternate Lesson 144

Let the sea resound,

and everything in it,

the world, and all who

live in it.

Psalm 98:7

Horizons® Penmanship Grade Two

Lessons 146 – 150: Review & Practice

Teaching Tips:

1. Quote for the week: **Psalm 98:8-9**.

2. Cursive alphabet review and practice: Lessons 146 – 147.

3. Trace and copy the letters while the teacher observes the position, formation and spacing.

4. Additional blank lines may be used for practice, for original sentences, for class sentences, for phrases, for rhyming words and so on.

5. Explain that the children will copy the verse from Lesson 149 onto the special page using their best handwriting skills.

6. Allow the children to practice on a separate sheet of paper.

7. Complete the final copy.

8. Decide how to use the special page.

Bible Verse Lessons 146-150

"Let the rivers clap their hands, let the mountain sing together for joy; let them sing before the Lord, for he comes to judge the earth."
(Psalm 98:8-9)

a b c d e f g

h i j k l m n

o p q r s t u

v w x y z

Let the rivers
clap their hands.
let the mountain
sing together for joy;
let them sing
before the Lord.
for he comes to
judge the earth.

Psalm 98:8-9

rivers clap

mountains sing

Lord comes

to judge the earth

Psalm 98:8-9

Alternate Lessons 146 - 149

Alternate Lesson 146

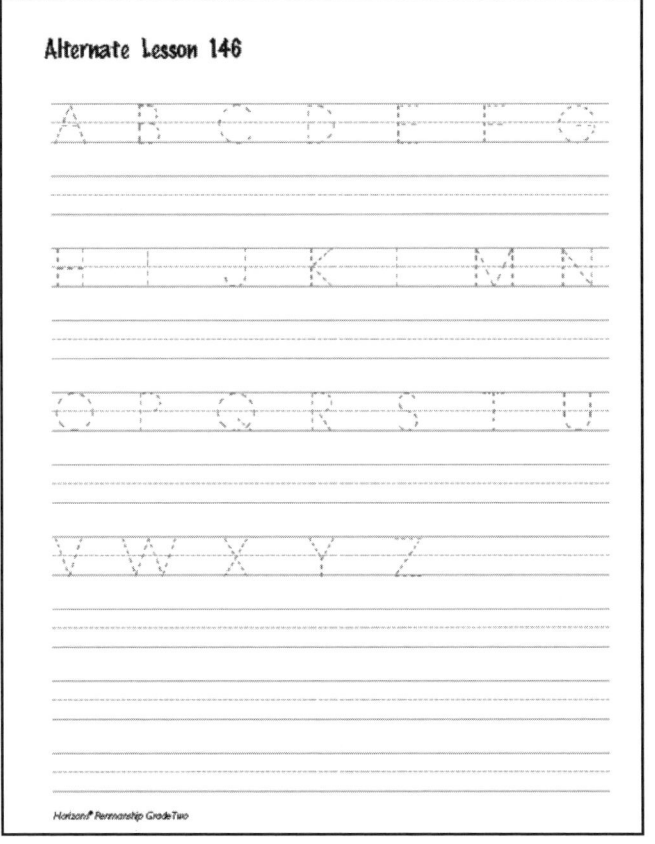

A B C D E F G

H I J K L M N

O P Q R S T U

V W X Y Z

Alternate Lesson 147

a b c d e f g

h i j k l m n

o p q r s t u

v w x y z

Alternate Lesson 148

rivers clap

mountains sing

lord comes

to judge the earth

Alternate Lesson 149

let the rivers clap their
hands.
let the mountain sing
together for joy.
let them sing before the
lord,
for he comes to judge
the earth.

Lesson 151 - Manuscript Writing Review

Teaching Tips:

1. Quote for the week: **Isaiah 2:2**.

2. Review and practice manuscript alphabet.

3. Watch formation and spacing.

4. Use the two blank lines at the bottom of the page to practice letters that need work.

Bible Verse Lessons 151-155

"The mountain of the Lord's temple will be established as chief among the mountians, it will be raised above the hills and all nations will stream to it." (Isaiah 2:2)

Lesson 152 - Manuscript Writing Review

Teaching Tips:

1. Write manuscript alphabet, both capital and lower case letters.

2. Note any continuing manuscript problems.

Bible Verse Lessons 151-155

"The mountain of the Lord's temple will be established as chief among the mountians, it will be raised above the hills and all nations will stream to it." (Isaiah 2:2)

Lesson 153 - Manuscript Writing Review

Teaching Tips:

1. Review verse for the week.

2. Practice words and phrases from verse.

3. Additional blank lines may be used for practice, for original sentences, for class sentences, for phrases, for rhyming words, for last name practice and so on.

Lesson 154 - Bible Verse

Teaching Tips:

1. Practice the verse
2. Practice writing the verse on a separate sheet of paper.

Bible Verse Lessons 151-155

"The mountain of the Lord's temple will be established as chief among the mountians, it will be raised above the hills, and all nations will stream to it." (Isaiah 2:2)

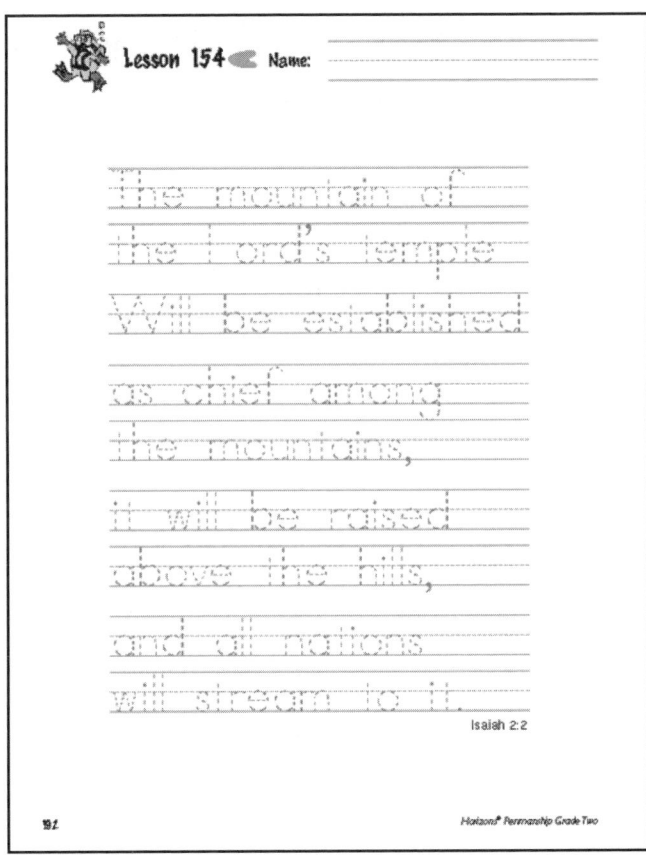

Lesson 155 - Special Page

Teaching Tips:

1. Explain that the children will copy the verse from Lesson 154 onto this special page using their best handwriting skills.

2. Allow the children to practice on the corresponding reproducible practice page from the back of this manual.

3. Complete the final copy allowing time because of the length of the verse.

4. Decide how this special page will be used.

Lesson 156 - Cursive Writing Review

Teaching Tips:

1. Quote for the week: **Psalm 150:1, 6.**
2. Final trace and practice of cursive alphabet.
3. Note any letters which still need work.
4. Watch formation and spacing.

Bible Verse Lessons 156-160

"Praise God in his sanctuary; praise him in his mighty heavens. Let everything that has breath praise the Lord."   (Psalm 150:1, 6)

Alternate Lesson 156 - Manuscript Writing Review

Teaching Tips:

1. Final trace and practice of manuscript alphabet.
2. Note any letters which still need work.
3. Watch formation and spacing.

Lesson 157 - Cursive Writing Review

Teaching Tips:

1. Read all of **Psalm 150**.
2. Children write their own cursive alphabet, both capital and lower case letters.

Bible Verse Lessons 156-160

"Praise God in his sanctuary; praise him in his mighty heavens. Let everything that has breath praise the Lord." (Psalm 150:1, 6)

Alternate Lesson 157 - Manuscript Writing Review

Teaching Tips:

1. Children write their own manuscript alphabet, both capital and lower case.

Lesson 158 - Cursive Writing Review

Teaching Tips:

1. Read **Psalm 150** as a class prayer.
2. Practice words and sentence.

Bible Verse Lessons 156-160

"Praise God in his sanctuary; praise him in his mighty heavens. Let everything that has breath praise the Lord." (Psalm 150:1, 6)

Lesson 158 Name:

sanctuary

mighty heavens

everything that

has breath

Praise the Lord.

197

Alternate Lesson 158 - Manuscript Writing Review

Teaching Tips:

1. Practice words and sentences.

Alternate Lesson 158

sanctuary

mighty heavens

everything that has

breath

Praise the Lord.

Lesson 159 - Bible Verse

Teaching Tips:

1. Read verses together.
2. Practice the verse.

Bible Verse Lessons 156-160

"Praise God in his sanctuary; praise him in his mighty heavens. Let everything that has breath praise the Lord." (Psalm 150:1, 6)

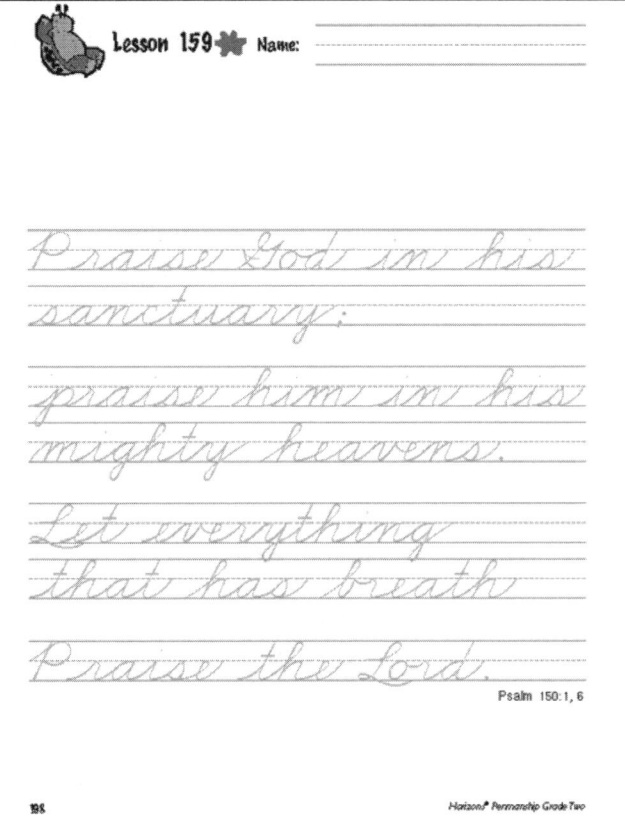

Alternate Lesson 159 - Bible Verse

Teaching Tips:

1. Practice the verse.

Lesson 160 - Special Page

Teaching Tips:

1. Explain that the children will copy the verse from Lesson 159 onto this special page using their best handwriting skills.

2. Allow the children to practice on the corresponding reproducible practice page from the back of this manual.

3. Complete the final copy of the verse.

4. Decide how this special page will be used.

Bible Verse Lessons 156-160

"Praise God in his sanctuary; praise him in his mighty heavens. Let everything that has breath praise the Lord." (Psalm 150:1, 6)

Lesson 5 Practice Page

Lesson 10   Practice Page

Lesson 15 Practice Page

Lesson 20   Practice Page

Lesson 30   Practice Page

Lesson 35   Practice Page

Psalm 147:7, 8-9

Who Has Seen the Wind?

The Wind

Lesson 50   Practice Page

Lesson 55 Practice Page

Lesson 60 Practice Page

Lesson 65   Practice Page

I Wandered Lonely as a Cloud

Lesson 70 Practice Page

Lesson 75   Practice Page

Song of Songs 2:11-12

Lesson 80 Practice Page

Psalm 23:1-2

Lesson 85   Practice Page

A. A. Milne

Lesson 90   Practice Page

Psalm 148:7-8

Lesson 95 Practice Page

Psalm 148:7, 9-10

When Fishes Set Umbrellas Up

Christina Rossetti

The Kitten and the Falling Leaves

William Wordsworth

Lesson 110   Practice Page

William Blake

The Eagle

Alfred, Lord Tennyson

A Bird Came Down the Walk

Emily Dickinson

Horizons Penmanship Grade 2

Lesson 125 Practice Page

William Wordsworth

Spring Morning

A. A. Milne

Lesson 140 Practice Page

Psalm 90:2

Lesson 145 Practice Page

Lesson 150   Practice Page

Psalm 98:8-9

Lesson 155   Practice Page

Isaiah 2:2

Lesson 160 Practice Page

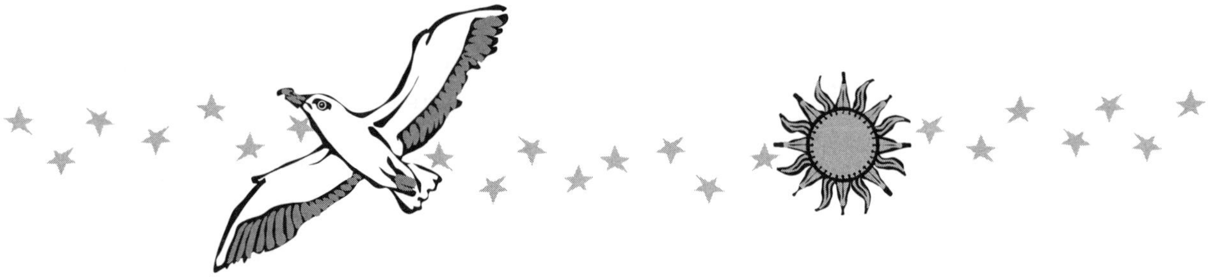

Psalm 150:1, 6

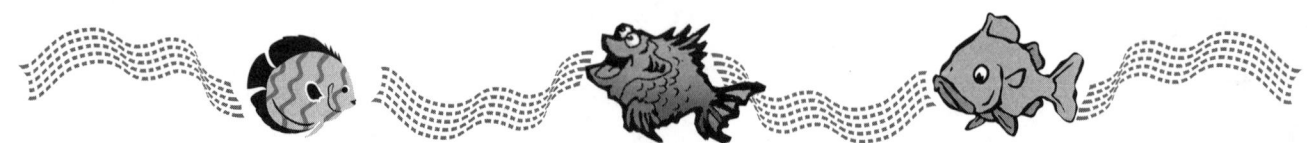

Alternate Lesson 76

shepherd

pastures

quiet

The Lord is my shepherd.

I shall not want.

He leads me.

He restores my soul.

I lie down.

I rest beside quiet waters

Alternate Lesson 81

anywhere

blue-bells

? ? ? ?

Alternate Lesson 82

Where am I going?

Where are you going?

What does it matter?

Alternate Lesson 83

Where do people go?

Where do blue-bells grow?

I don't know.

Alternate Lesson 86

sea creatures

ocean depths

lightning and hail

Alternate Lesson 87

snow and clouds

stormy winds

do his bidding

Alternate Lesson 88

Praise the Lord from

the earth.

Things of the earth

that praise the Lord.

Alternate Lesson 91

fruit trees and cedars

wild animals

cattle

Alternate Lesson 92

small creatures

flying birds

all the hills

Alternate Lesson 93

I praise the Lord.

All creation praises the Lord.

How do you praise the Lord?

rain-drops

umbrellas

parasols

Alternate Lesson 97

lizards

shade

from the sun

Alternate Lesson 98

Umbrellas keep us dry.

Parasols keep the sun

off of us.

Have you seen a lizard

with a parasol?

Alternate Lesson 101

withered leaves

elder trees

frosty air

Alternate Lesson 102

See the kitten

sporting with leaves.

through the calm and

frosty air

Alternate Lesson 103

one, two, and three

Of the morning bright

and fair

Alternate Lesson 106

Tiger! Tiger!

burning bright

forests of the night

Alternate Lesson 107

immortal hand

fearful symmetry

William Blake

Alternate Lesson 108

fearful

night

bright

hand

could

Alternate Lesson 111

crooked hands

clasps the crag

close to the sun

Alternate Lesson 112

azure world

wrinkled sea

ringed the world

Alternate Lesson 113

mountain walls,

thunderbolt

He watches and falls

Alternate Lesson 116

A Bird Came Down the

Walk

Emily

Dickinson

halves

fellow

worm

Alternate Lesson 118

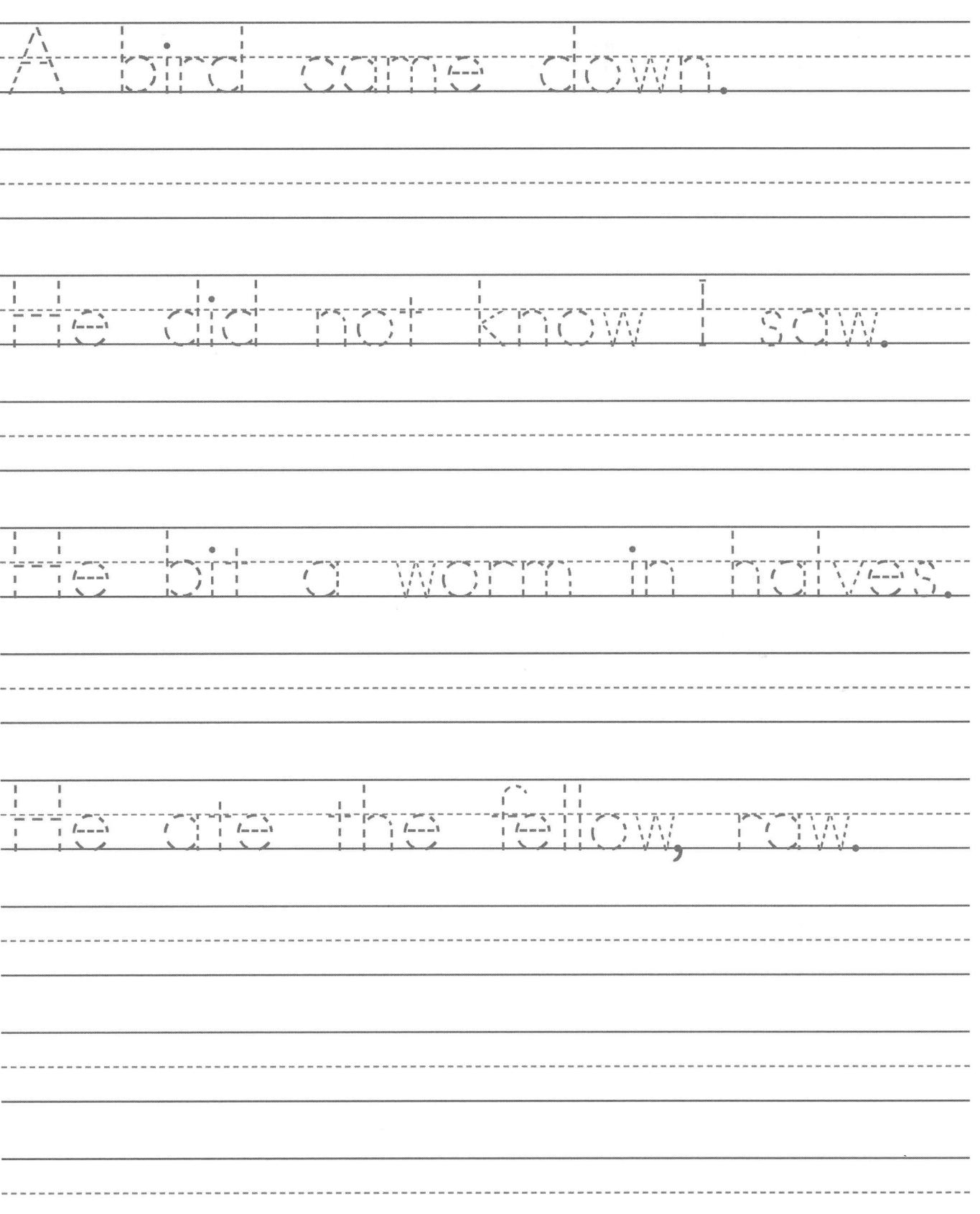

A bird came down.

He did not know I saw.

He bit a worm in halves.

He ate the fellow, raw.

Alternate Lesson 119

A Bird Came Down the Walk

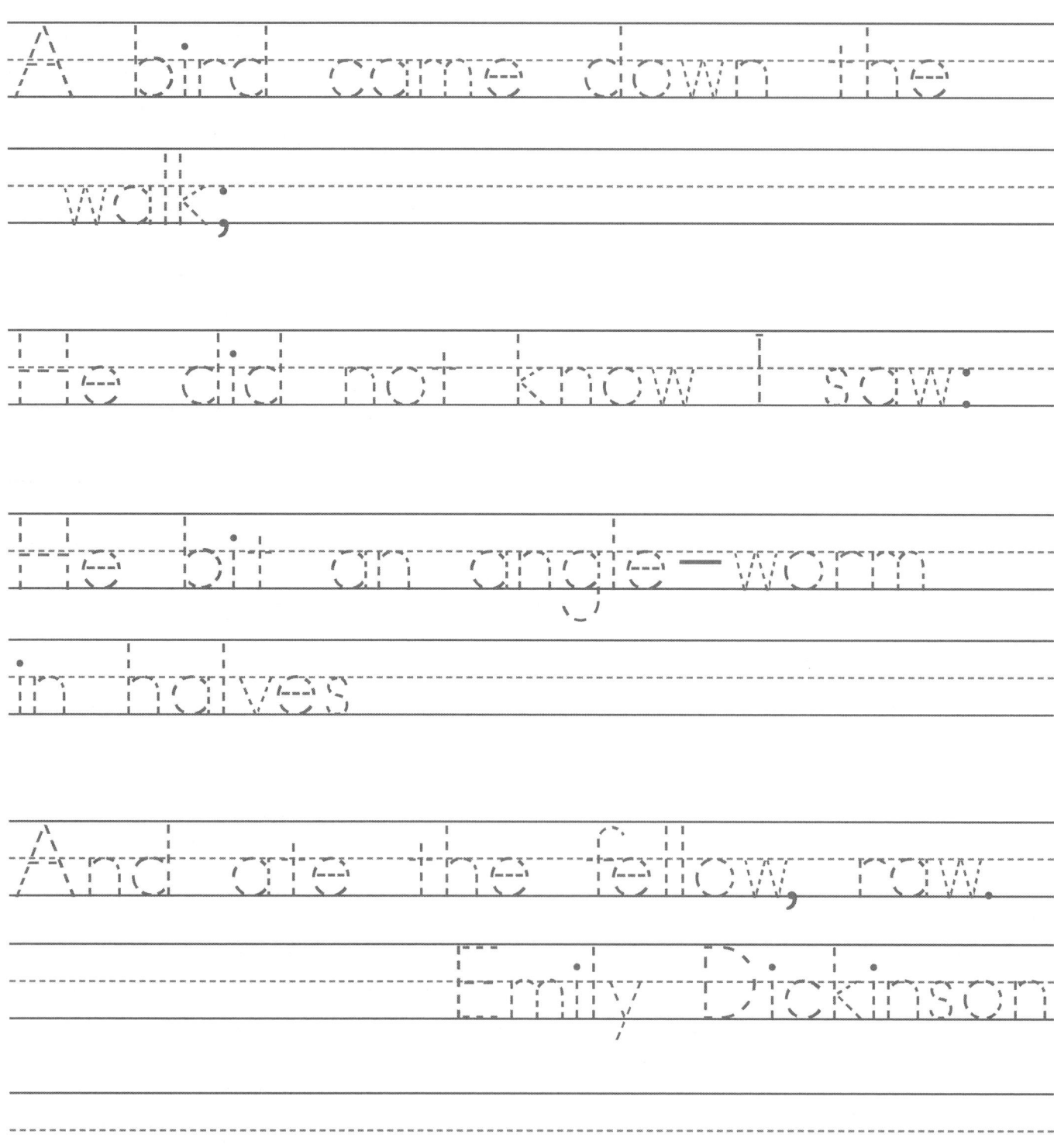

A bird came down the

walk;

He did not know I saw.

He bit an angle-worm

in halves

And ate the fellow, raw.

Emily Dickinson

Alternate Lesson 121

crowing

flowing

green field steeps

written

Alternate Lesson 122

twitter

glitter

stream

March

Alternate Lesson 123

The cock is crowing. The

stream is flowing. The

small birds twitter. The

lake doth glitter. The green

field sleeps in the sun.

Alternate Lesson 124

Written in March

The cock is crowing,

The stream is flowing,

The small birds twitter,

The lake doth glitter,

The green field sleeps in

the sun.

Alternate Lesson 126

you'd

that's

Alternate Lesson 127

A bird can fly.

Can you fly?

What do you want to

do?

If I were a bird, and

lived on high, and

"That's where I wanted

to go today."

A. A. Milne

Alternate Lesson 129

If you were a bird, and

lived on high,

You'd lean on the wind

when the wind came by,

You'd say to the wind

when it took you away:

"That's where I wanted

to go today!"

A. A. Milne

T   T   There's

S   S   Small

B   B   Blue

W   W   William

mountains

fountains

sailing

prevailing

Alternate Lesson 133

rain is over

joy

life

Wordsworth

Alternate Lesson 134

There's joy in the
mountains;

There's life in the
fountains;

Small clouds are sailing,

Blue sky prevailing;

The rain is over and
gone !

Wordsworth

Lord

God

Psalm

born

Alternate Lesson 137

brought forth

the earth

the world

everlasting

Alternate Lesson 138

You are God. You

brought forth the

earth. You brought

forth the world.

You are everlasting.

Alternate Lesson 139

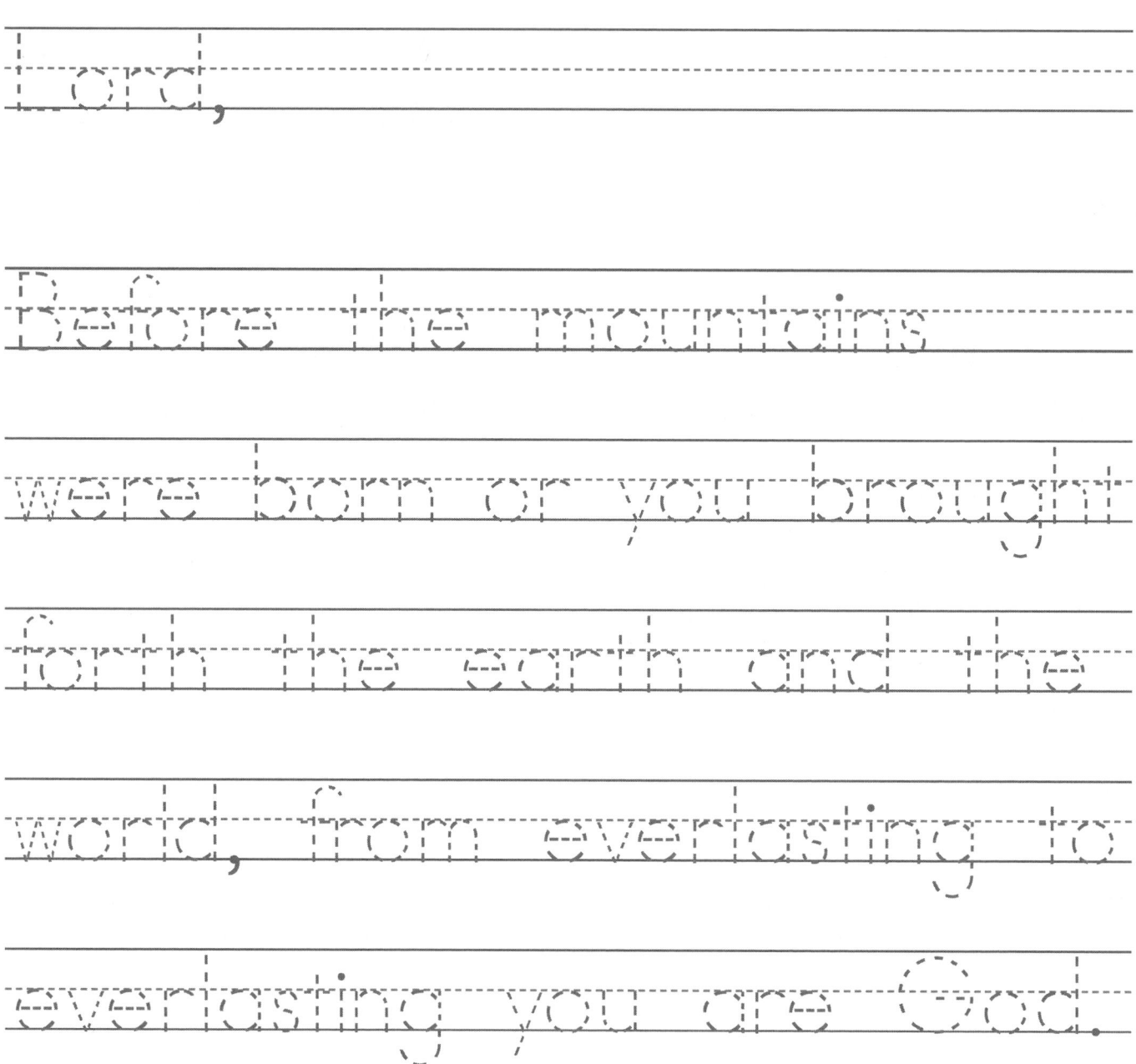

Lord,

Before the mountains

were born or you brought

forth the earth and the

world, from everlasting to

everlasting you are God.

Psalm 90:2

Horizons Penmanship Grade Two

Alternate Lesson 141

A a   B b

C c   D d

E e   F f

G g   H h

I i   J j

Alternate Lesson 142

K k   L l

M m   N n

O o   P p

Q q   R r

S s   T t

Alternate Lesson 143

U u   V v

W w   X x

Y y   Z z

resound

everything

Alternate Lesson 144

Let the sea resound,

and everything in it,

the world, and all who

live in it.

Psalm 98:7

Alternate Lesson 146

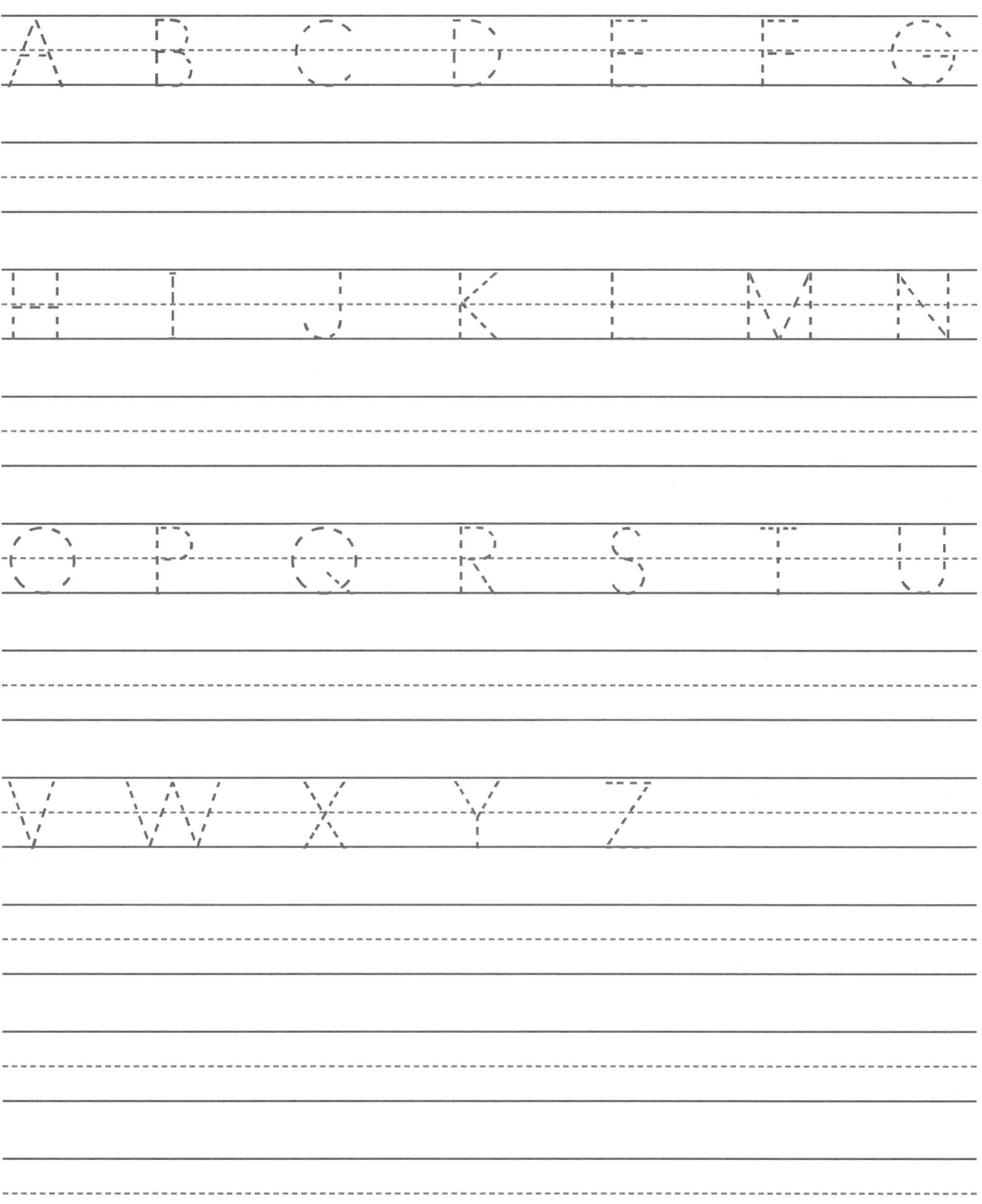

Alternate Lesson 147

a   b   c   d   e   f   g

h   i   j   k   l   m   n

o   p   q   r   s   t   u

v   w   x   y   z

Horizons Penmanship Grade Two

Alternate Lesson 148

rivers clap

mountains sing

Lord comes

to judge the earth

Alternate Lesson 149

Let the rivers clap their
hands.

Let the mountain sing
together for joy;

let them sing before the
Lord,

for he comes to judge
the earth.

Alternate Lesson 156

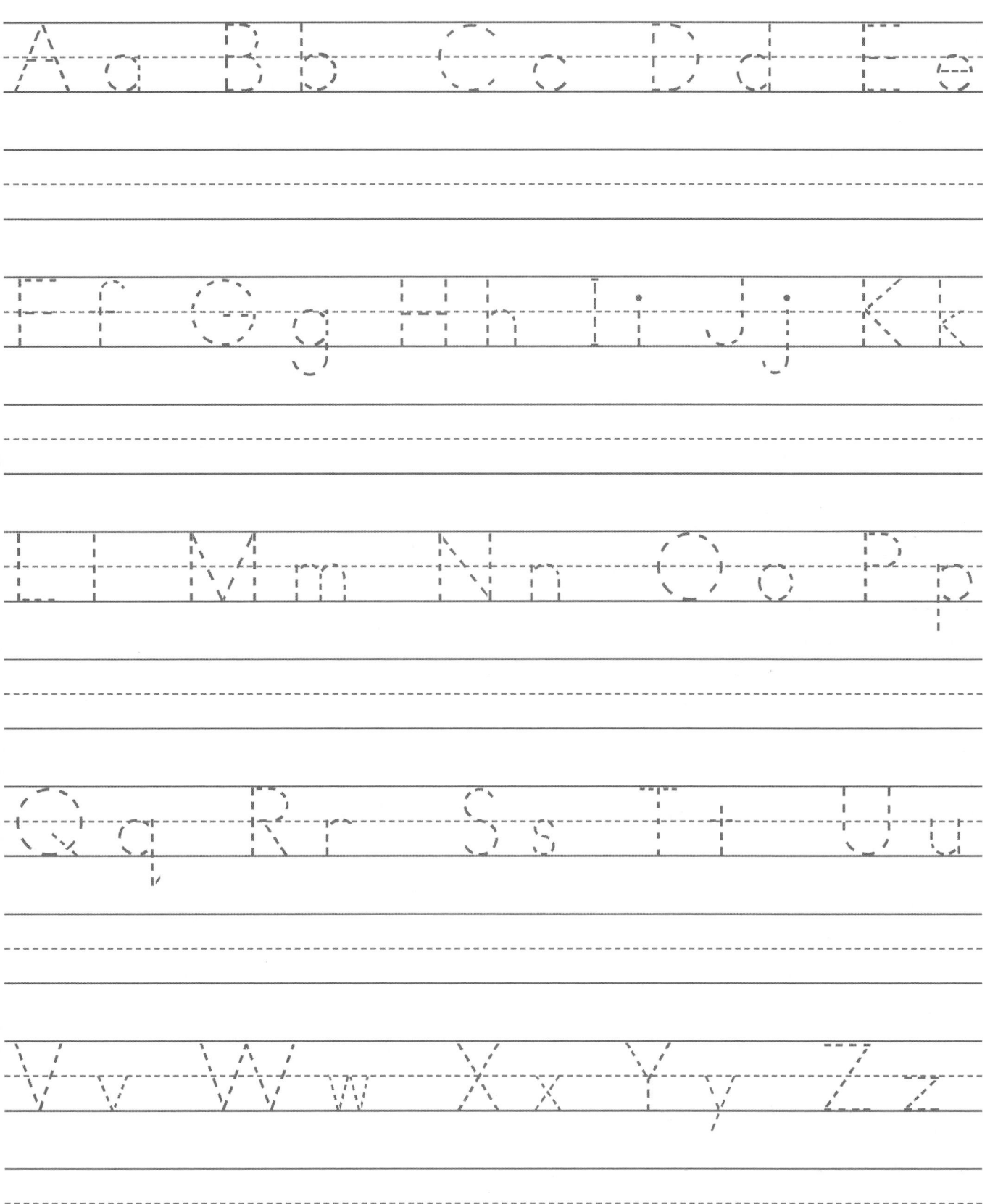

Alternate Lesson 158

sanctuary

mighty heavens

everything that has

breath

Praise the Lord.

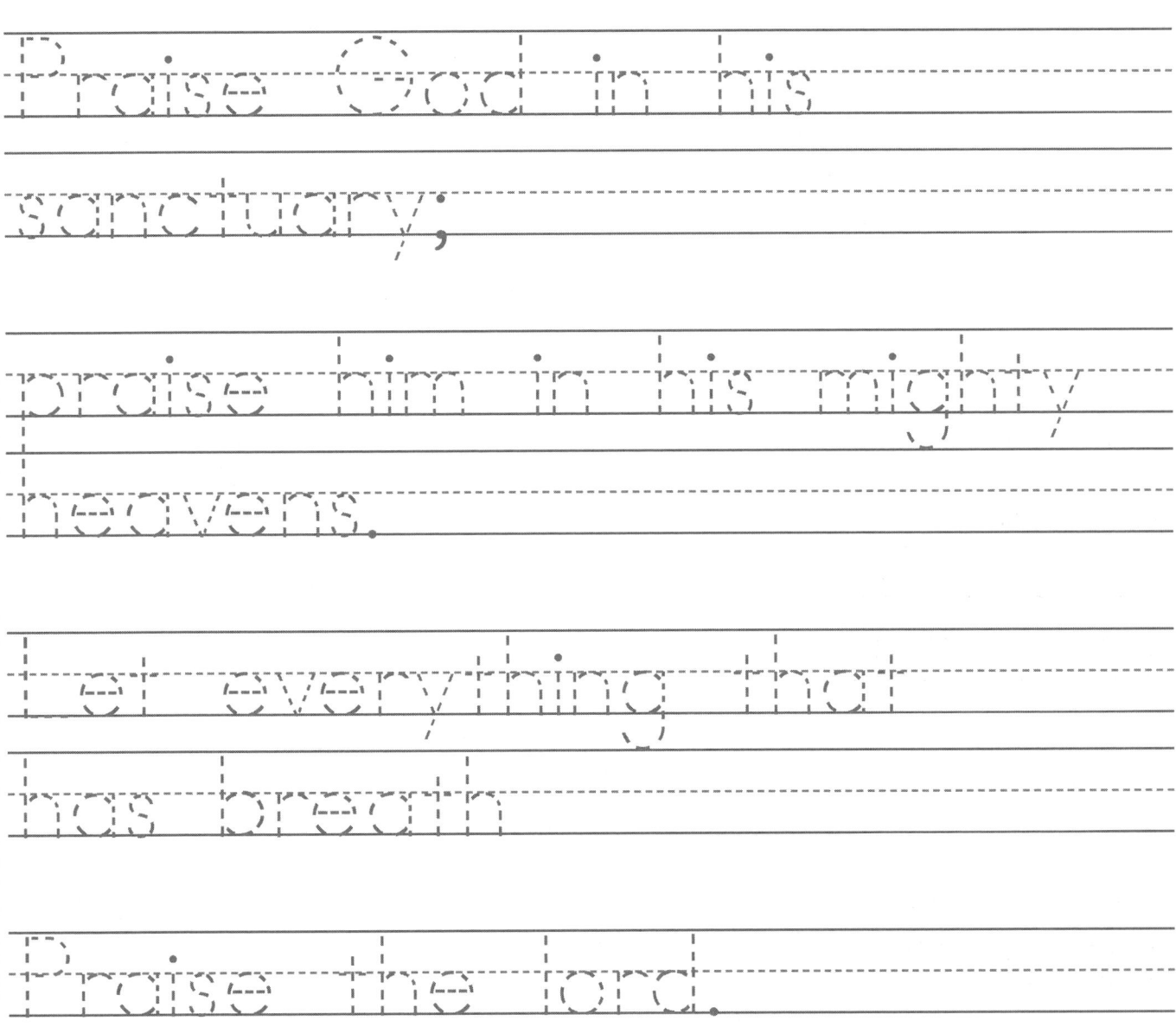

Praise God in his
sanctuary;

praise him in his mighty
heavens.

Let everything that
has breath

Praise the lord.

Psalm 150:1, 6

Alternate Lesson